Exam Ref MS-700 Managing Microsoft Teams

Ed Fisher

Exam Ref MS-700 Managing Microsoft Teams

Published with the authorization of Microsoft Corporation by:
Pearson Education, Inc.

ISBN-13: 978-0-13-757872-6
ISBN-10: 0-13-757872-5

Library of Congress Control Number: 2021946890

1 2021

TRADEMARKS

WARNING AND DISCLAIMER

SPECIAL SALES

For information about buying this title in bulk quantities, or for special sales opportunities (which may include electronic versions; custom cover designs; and content particular to your business, training goals, marketing focus, or branding interests), please contact our corporate sales department at corpsales@pearsoned.com or (800) 382-3419.

For government sales inquiries, please contact governmentsales@pearsoned.com.

For questions about sales outside the U.S., please contact intlcs@pearson.com.

CREDITS

EDITOR-IN-CHIEF
Brett Bartow

EXECUTIVE EDITOR
Loretta Yates

SPONSORING EDITOR
Charvi Arora

DEVELOPMENT EDITOR
Songlin Qiu

MANAGING EDITOR
Sandra Schroeder

SENIOR PROJECT EDITOR
Tracey Croom

COPY EDITOR
Liz Welch

INDEXER
Ken Johnson

PROOFREADER
Abigail Manheim

TECHNICAL EDITOR
Chris L'Hommedieu

EDITORIAL ASSISTANT
Cindy Teeters

COVER DESIGNER
Twist Creative, Seattle

COMPOSITOR
codeMantra

I dedicate this book to my wife Connie, who gave me the time, encouragement, and support to do this all again.

—ED FISHER

Contents at a glance

Contents

Chapter 3   Manage Teams and app policies   129

Acknowledgments

I'd like to thank the following people for being a part of this work, whether or not they realized it at the time. My fantastic team at Pearson, especially Loretta Yates, Charvi Arora, Tracey Croom, and Liz Welch. You have been incredible to work with and truly made my efforts easier. My comrade-in-arms, Chris L'Hommedieu, whose technical edits and suggestions greatly improved this book. My manager, Shahira Scott, who supported my taking on this project, and finally both Arjun Dabir and Jeffrey Strasser, who supported my move from Security to Teams, even though things didn't shake out the way any of us expected. Thank you all.

About the author

ED FISHER is a Principal Technical Specialist at Microsoft, currently covering Microsoft Teams. He's been with Microsoft for over 10 years, in various roles, all covering some aspect of Microsoft 365. A former bean counter, in 1997 he figured out that IT is way more interesting than balance sheets and has been a self-professed geek ever since. You can reach out at *https://aka.ms/edfisher.*

Introduction

Most books take a very low-level approach, teaching you how to use individual classes and accomplish fine-grained tasks. Like the Microsoft MS-700 certification exam, this book takes a high-level approach, building on your knowledge of and experience with administering Microsoft Teams, extending that into every area covered by the exam, including those not everyone currently using Microsoft Teams may have touched.

This book covers every major topic area found on the exam, but it does not cover every exam question. Only the Microsoft exam team has access to the exam questions, and Microsoft regularly adds new questions to the exam, making it impossible to cover specific questions. You should consider this book a supplement to your relevant real-world experience and other study materials. If you encounter a topic in this book that you do not feel completely comfortable with, use the "Need more review?" links you'll find in the text to find more information and take the time to research and study the topic. Great information is available online in docs. microsoft.com, and in blogs and forums.

Organization of this book

This book is organized by the "Skills measured" list published for the exam. The "Skills measured" list is available for each exam on the Microsoft Learn website: *http://aka.ms/examlist*. Each chapter in this book corresponds to a major topic area in the list, and the technical tasks in each topic area determine a chapter's organization. If an exam covers six major topic areas, for example, the book will contain six chapters.

Preparing for the exam

Microsoft certification exams are a great way to build your résumé and let the world know about your level of expertise. Certification exams validate your on-the-job experience and product knowledge. Although there is no substitute for on-the-job experience, preparation through study and hands-on practice can help you prepare for the exam. This book is *not* designed to teach you new skills.

We recommend that you augment your exam preparation plan by using a combination of available study materials and courses. For example, you might use the Exam Ref and another study guide for your "at home" preparation and take a Microsoft Official Curriculum course for the classroom experience. Choose the combination that you think works best for you. Learn more about available classroom training and find free online courses and live events at *http://microsoft.com/learn*. Microsoft Official Practice Tests are available for many exams at *http://aka.ms/practicetests*.

Note that this Exam Ref is based on publicly available information about the exam and the author's experience. To safeguard the integrity of the exam, authors do not have access to the live exam.

Microsoft certifications

Microsoft certifications distinguish you by proving your command of a broad set of skills and experience with current Microsoft products and technologies. The exams and corresponding certifications are developed to validate your mastery of critical competencies as you design and develop, or implement and support, solutions with Microsoft products and technologies both on-premises and in the cloud. Certification brings a variety of benefits to the individual and to employers and organizations.

> **NEED MORE REVIEW? ALL MICROSOFT CERTIFICATIONS**
>
> For information about Microsoft certifications, including a full list of available certifications, go to *http://www.microsoft.com/learn*.

Check back often to see what is new!

Quick access to online references

Throughout this book are addresses to webpages that the author has recommended you visit for more information. Some of these links can be very long and painstaking to type, so we've shortened them for you to make them easier to visit. We've also compiled them into a single list that readers of the print edition can refer to while they read.

Download the list at *MicrosoftPressStore.com/ExamRefMS700/downloads*.

The URLs are organized by chapter and heading. Every time you come across a URL in the book, find the hyperlink in the list to go directly to the webpage.

Errata, updates, & book support

We've made every effort to ensure the accuracy of this book and its companion content. You can access updates to this book—in the form of a list of submitted errata and their related corrections—at:

MicrosoftPressStore.com/ExamRefMS700/errata.

If you discover an error that is not already listed, please submit it to us at the same page.

For additional book support and information, please visit

MicrosoftPressStore.com/Support.

Please note that product support for Microsoft software and hardware is not offered through the previous addresses. For help with Microsoft software or hardware, go to *http://support.microsoft.com.*

Stay in touch

Let's keep the conversation going! We're on Twitter: *http://twitter.com/MicrosoftPress.*

CHAPTER 1

Plan and configure a Microsoft Teams environment

In this first chapter, we cover some fundamental aspects of administering Microsoft Teams, including content for new deployments as well as for upgrades from Skype for Business Online. Based on the current exam objectives, this chapter includes the content that accounts for somewhere beween 45% and 50% of what will be in the exam, so let's dive right in.

Skills covered in this chapter:

- Skill 1.1: Upgrade from Skype for Business to Microsoft Teams
- Skill 1.2: Plan and configure network settings for Microsoft Teams
- Skill 1.3: Implement governance and lifecycle management for Microsoft Teams
- Skill 1.4: Configure and manage guest access
- Skill 1.5: Manage security and compliance
- Skill 1.6: Deploy and manage Microsoft Teams endpoints
- Skill 1.7: Monitor and analyze service usage

Skill 1.1: Upgrade from Skype for Business to Microsoft Teams

It's worth noting that although support for Skype for Business Online ends in July 2021, Skype for Business can be deployed on-premises, and you may still encounter situations where you will need to migrate users from an on-prem environment to Microsoft Teams. Even if your organization is completely on Microsoft Teams today, pay close attention to this topic—you may see a lot of questions on the exam about this.

> **This skill covers how to:**
> - Choose an appropriate upgrade path and coexistence mode to meet specific requirements
> - Plan and troubleshoot meeting migration
> - Configure Microsoft Teams upgrade notification and meeting app preferences
> - Configure coexistence mode for the organization and per-user
> - Use Teams Advisor to assess and identify steps to roll out Microsoft Teams

Choose an appropriate upgrade path and coexistence mode to meet specific requirements

Migrating from Skype for Business to Microsoft Teams can be straightforward when you are moving from Skype for Business Online to Microsoft Teams, but the migration requires more planning and effort when you are moving from Skype for Business on-premises. Most organizations require some degree of coexistence and need to minimize user disruptions during the process. You must determine the appropriate coexistence mode for your users, how you wish to upgrade, and the timelines to support both the business and your users' training needs.

Let's address coexistence first. The good news is that you can take your time, and even have both Skype for Business and Teams in your environment. Users can use both Skype for Business (on-premises or online) and Microsoft Teams at the same time, running both clients on the same machine. The coexistence modes determine which functions are handled by each client and service and which options are presented to the end user in each client. Coexistence modes include the following, detailed in Table 1-1.

TABLE 1-1 Coexistence modes

Coexistence mode	Details
SfBOnly	Users run only the Skype for Business (SfB) client. They can - Initiate chats and calls only from the SfB client, no matter what the other party is using - Receive chats and calls only in the SfB client, no matter what the other party is using - Only schedule SfB meetings - Attend both SfB and Teams meetings scheduled by others - Not have some on-prem users in SfBOnly mode and others in Islands mode, because the on-prem SfBOnly users may be unreachable to the Teams users
SfBWithTeamsCollab	Users run both the SfB and Teams clients. They can - Use all the existing functionality available to them in SfB - Use Teams for group collaboration in channels - Not use Teams for chat, calling, or meeting scheduling, because those features are disabled in the client

Coexistence mode	Details
SfBWithTeams CollabAndMeetings	Users also run both the SfB and Teams clients. They can ■ Use SfB for chat and calling ■ Use Teams for group collaboration, including channel conversations, but not for 1:1 chat or calling ■ Only schedule Teams meetings, but can attend both SfB and Teams meetings scheduled by others
Islands (Default)	Users again run both the SfB and Teams clients. They can ■ Initiate chats and VoIP calls using either client, but if they are homed on-premises, they cannot use Teams to reach another SfBOnly user. They must use the SfB client for that. ■ Receive chats and calls in the same client that the caller used to initiate the chat or call, *if in the same tenant*. ■ Receive chats and calls in the Teams client if the user using SfB client is *in a federated tenant* ■ Use SfB client for PSTN calls, whether homed on-premises or in Skype for Business Online ■ Schedule and attend meetings using either client, but cannot schedule in one and then attend in the other
Teams Only	Users run only the Microsoft Teams client. They can ■ Initiate and receive chats and calls in the Teams client, regardless of which client the other party is using ■ Schedule Teams meetings only, though they can still join Skype for Business meetings scheduled by others

Coexistence mode is controlled by the TeamsUpgradePolicy and ultimately determines three things:

■ To which client application incoming chats and calls are delivered

■ Which client application users use to initiate chats and calls

■ In which service meetings are scheduled

Coexistence mode is set for users, using either the Teams admin center (TAC) or Power-Shell. All modes except for Teams Only mode can be assigned to on-premises users. You can also set a tenant-wide default that will apply to all users, and then set per-user to override the tenant-wide setting.

To set Coexistence mode in the TAC, do the following:

1. If necessary, open the TAC by browsing to *https://admin.teams.microsoft.com* and authenticating as either a Global Administrator or a Teams administrator.

2. In the left menu, select **Users**, then select the user from the list you wish to modify.

3. On the **Account** tab, scroll down to **Teams upgrade**, and select **Edit**.

4. Set the desired **Coexistence mode**.

5. (Recommended, optional) Enable notifications so that the user will see a banner in their Skype for Business client.

6. Select **Save**, as shown in Figure 1-1.

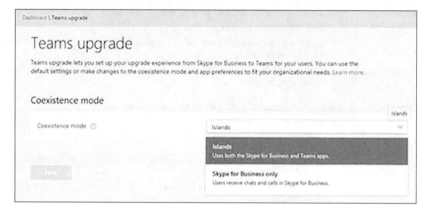

FIGURE 1-1 The Coexistence Mode settings for a user in the TAC

If you do not set a coexistence mode for individual users, then the Org-wide Settings will apply to all users, as shown in Figure 1-2.

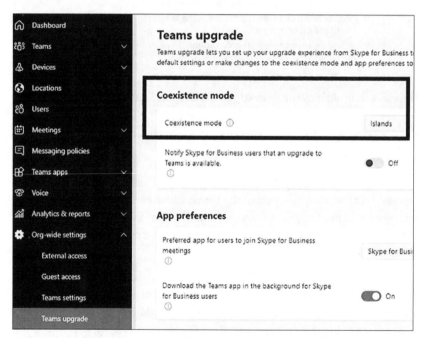

FIGURE 1-2 The Coexistence mode settings for all users

You can also control these settings using PowerShell and the **Grant-CsTeamsUpgradePolicy** cmdlet from the Skype for Business PowerShell module. See *https://docs.microsoft.com/en-us/powershell/module/skype/grant-csteamsupgradepolicy?view=skype-ps* for more information on using PowerShell to control these settings.

Be careful when using more than one mode with your users. If a Teams Only user tries to connect to an Islands mode user, and that user is only running the Skype for Business client, they will be unreachable and appear as offline to the Teams Only user. You may test functionality with small groups of pilot users, but don't roll out changes to large numbers of regular users until you set appropriate expectations with others and the help desk is ready to provide appropriate support.

EXAM TIP

The difference between what an Islands user can receive depending on whether the initiator is in the same tenant or a federated one is just the sort of thing you may see again on the exam. Be sure you know the difference!

NEED MORE REVIEW? **COEXISTENCE SPELLED OUT**

You can read more about coexistence modes at *https://docs.microsoft.com/en-us/ microsoftteams/teams-and-skypeforbusiness-coexistence-and-interoperability.*

Upgrading from Skype for Business Online to Microsoft Teams is relatively easy since both services are in the cloud. Upgrading from Skype for Business on-premises to Microsoft Teams can be done as a cutover, but the user impact could be significant there. Therefore, establishing hybrid connectivity and migrating users while maintaining contact lists, and updating meeting invites, is a much smoother way to go.

When planning an upgrade from either Skype for Business on-premises (SfB) or Skype for Business Online (SfBO), you must keep in mind these important points. First, Teams Only mode means that a user has either been completely upgraded from SfB or SfBO to Teams, or they were provisioned directly into Teams. They have no services being provided by SfB or SfBO. That said, meetings are joined using the client associated with the service where the meeting was created by the meeting organizer. If an SfBO user creates a meeting in SfBO and invites a Teams Only user to join the meeting, when the Teams Only user joins, they will use the SfB client to do so.

You also need to consider the potential productivity impact to the user when upgrading and not only the technical aspects. User awareness and training are both important, so do not overlook the change management aspects of the upgrade. Make sure that you are addressing users, use cases, hardware and software, and support needs. The upgrade should start with a proven framework, such as the one provided by Microsoft at *https://aka.ms/SkypeToTeams.*

Because user adoption is the most important part of this upgrade, running SfB/SfBO and Microsoft Teams side by side is preferable to simply cutting users over. Running them side by side gives users the chance to become familiar with the new capabilities in Teams while not being forced to change what they are already used to doing in SfB/SfBO.

Technical readiness is also critical. In addition to ensuring that you can deploy the client software, that your admins and your support staff are all trained and ready to help your end users, and that any calling/meeting hardware is compatible, you must ensure that your network is ready to go. Customers currently using Skype for Business on-premises will be moving significant traffic from their on-prem environment to the cloud. If this is your situation, you should invest time to make sure your network is healthy and ready for Microsoft Teams. In addition to ensuring that you have reviewed and implemented the guidance for connecting to Microsoft's cloud services documented at *https://aka.ms/pnc*, you should use the Network planner tools available in the TAC to evaluate available bandwidth and determine whether upgrades are needed. You can monitor pilot users with the Call Quality Dashboard and Call Analytics, which will be covered later in this chapter in Skill 1.7.

The target end state of an upgrade from SfB or SfBO to Microsoft Teams is to get to Teams Only mode for all users. All features and capabilities available to users are in Microsoft Teams, and the user no longer needs to launch the Skype for Business client except to join an SfB meeting. Users' contact lists are maintained, and existing meetings a user scheduled in SfB are automatically updated to use Microsoft Teams. If a user tries to launch the Skype for Business client, they will be prompted to launch Teams, and the Skype for Business client will only show them their calendar with SfB meetings that already exist.

When you are ready to upgrade, you can choose between two options. The first is to go directly from Skype for Business to Teams Only mode. The second is to run Skype for Business and Teams together using one of the coexistence modes discussed previously.

Table 1-2 summarizes the upgrade paths available, with some of the pros and cons for each.

TABLE 1-2 Upgrade paths

Upgrade mode	Pros	Cons
Full side-by-side approach ■ Relies on adoption and change management (ACM). ■ Is fast, but also may be impactful to end users. ■ The upgrade completes when ACM determines that the org is ready.	Users get the full Teams experience immediately. Users can continue to use the SfB client when they prefer. Fastest path to retiring SfB/SfBO.	Users must run both clients concurrently. No interoperability between the services. Federation requires users to continue to use SfB. Some users may be "stranded" or find others unreachable unless they use the correct client.
Side-by-side with interop ■ IT sets dates. ■ Decouples the upgrade from adoption saturation. ■ Useful if some compliance, legacy, or Enterprise Voice requirements mean some on-premises will have to remain.	Supports legacy requirements. Provides more time to migrate calling capabilities. User starts with all chat/meetings/calling capabilities still in SfB, while collaboration is introduced in Teams. Allows the org to pilot capabilities with users.	Not all features will be available in Teams, reducing the overall experience for users.

When you are upgrading from Skype for Business on-premises to Microsoft Teams, the most critical component of all is to have Azure Active Directory Connect (AADConnect) properly set up and configured to synchronize users from the on-prem environment to Office 365. You must ensure proper sync is in place before creating the first Teams user. Coverage of AADConnect is beyond the scope of this book, but you can read more at *https://aka.ms/ TeamsAADConnect*.

You also want to ensure that Skype for Business Hybrid is set up so that you can migrate users' settings from the on-prem environment to Microsoft Teams, share a Session Initiation Protocol (SIP) namespace, and enable users in both Microsoft Teams and Skype for Business to communicate. Hybrid between Skype for Business and either Skype for Business Online or Microsoft Teams relies on AADConnect properly synchronizing users and attributes and the sharing of a SIP namespace (the DNS domain name you are using for SIP). In addition, the on-premises organization must meet the following infrastructure requirements:

- A single deployment of Skype for Business on-premises running either Skype for Business Server 2019 or Skype for Business Server 2015, or a single deployment of Microsoft Lync Server 2013. If hybrid voice is required, you must introduce either Skype for Business Server 2015 or Skype for Business Server 2019 (but not both) into the on-premises org as the Federation Edge as well as the pool associated with the SIP federation, before proceeding.

- A single Microsoft 365 organization with Skype for Business Online enabled, and licenses for both Skype for Business Online and Microsoft Teams.

- AADConnect properly synchronizing users.

- You must enable a shared SIP address space in your on-premises environment.

- You must configure the Microsoft 365 organization as a hosting provider within your on-premises environment.

- You must use Open Federation (federation that uses SRV DNS record lookups) both for hybrid connectivity and to maintain federation with any external partners or customers. If your on-premises organization currently uses closed federation (using a fixed IP address or fully qualified domain name [FQDN] to define the endpoint), you must migrate to Open Federation first. This may interrupt federation with external parties, so review your federation relationships and update your partners if necessary.

NEED MORE REVIEW?   SETTING UP HYBRID

See *https://aka.ms/TeamsSFBHybrid* for more information on setting up Skype for Business Hybrid with Microsoft Teams.

Plan and troubleshoot meeting migration

When you are upgrading from Skype for Business (SfB) or Skype for Business Online (SfBO) to Microsoft Teams, one of the biggest changes will be to existing/recurring meetings in users' schedules. Skype for Business Hybrid enables you to migrate meetings, updating them from Skype for Business to Microsoft Teams. The Meeting Migration Service (MMS) performs this automatically for users by default whenever they are moved from on-premises to online, or from any Skype coexistence mode to either TeamsOnly or SfBwithTeamsCollabAndMeetings. The Meeting Migration Service does require that the user's mailbox be hosted in Exchange Online, and it is a one-way update from either Skype for Business on-premises to online or from Skype for Business Online to Microsoft Teams. If you move a user and decide you need to move them back, you will have to update (or delete and re-create) meetings manually.

There are several caveats/limitations to the MMS that you should be aware of when moving users. These are very important to consider when planning your moves, as well as when you are troubleshooting if a meeting did not get updated or some changes were made that you did not expect. Be sure you are aware, and consider the impacts of, the following:

- When the MMS updates a meeting, it replaces everything in the meeting invite, including comments and agenda. The updated meeting will contain only the actual meeting link, time, and (if relevant) dial-in details.

- Only meetings that were originally scheduled using the **Add Skype Meeting** plug-in in Outlook, or using the functionality in Outlook Web App (OWA), will be updated. If a user created a meeting and manually copied join information into the invite, it will not be updated.

- Content attached to meeting invites such as whiteboards or polls or files will be dropped.

- Meetings with more than 250 attendees will not be updated.

- Meeting titles with UNICODE characters may see glitches in the text after the MMS runs.

- Updates will not occur until two hours or so have passed since the user was moved. If any errors are encountered, the MMS will retry over the next 24 hours. Keep that timing in mind when scheduling moves.

After you've moved a user from Skype for Business on-prem to the cloud, or updated a user's coexistence mode to SfBWithTeamsCollabAndMeetings or TeamsOnly, or updated a user's Audio Conferencing settings, the MMS will run (unless you disable it). If you have any problems with a meeting being updated, the issue is likely related to one of the previous caveats. You can disable the Meeting Migration Service by running the PowerShell cmdlet **Set-CsOnlineDialInConferencingTenantSettings -AutomaticallyMigrateUserMeetings $false**.

Configure Microsoft Teams upgrade notification and meeting app preferences

When you are upgrading from Skype for Business or Skype for Business Online to Microsoft Teams, user communications will be very important. In addition to any change management processes that you have in place or end-user training, you can directly notify users in the Skype for Business client that the upgrade is coming.

You can enable a banner to appear in the Skype for Business client so that when a user launches or uses the Skype for Business client, they will see a notification in the client, as shown in Figure 1-3.

FIGURE 1-3 The notification banner in the Skype for Business client

To enable the option "Notify Skype for Business users that Teams is available for upgrade" do the following:

1. Log on to the TAC at *https://admin.teams.microsoft.com*.
2. In the left menu, select **Org-wide settings** and then **Teams upgrade**.
3. Set the coexistence mode you want to use.
4. Set **Notify Skype for Business users that Teams is available for upgrade** to **On**.
   To set the meeting app preferences, continue as follows:
5. Specify whether users with Teams join Skype meetings using the full Skype for Business client or the Skype Meetings app and whether or not the Teams app should be downloaded in the background so that Skype for Business users have the client when they are ready to start using Teams.
6. Select **Save**.

Configure coexistence mode for the organization and per-user

Coexistence mode can be set for the entire organization by specifying it in the Org-wide Settings. Users will inherit this setting and have the coexistence experience you set, unless you specify the setting on a per-user basis. Doing so enables you to set a default experience, and to test a different setting for a subset of users or provide an exception for specific use cases. As in the previous section, you set the org-wide coexistence mode as follows:

1. Log on to the TAC at *https://admin.teams.microsoft.com.*

2. In the left menu, select **Org-wide Settings** and then **Teams upgrade**.

3. Set the coexistence mode you want to use. The options are as follows:

   a. **Islands**—Use this setting if you want users to be able to use both Skype for Business and Teams simultaneously.

   b. **Skype for Business only**—Use this setting if you want your users to only use Skype for Business.

   c. **Skype for Business with Teams collaboration**—Use this setting if you want your users to use Skype for Business in addition to using Teams for group collaboration (channels).

   d. **Skype for Business with Teams collaboration and meetings**—Use this setting if you want your users to use Skype for Business in addition to using Teams for group collaboration (channels) and Teams meetings.

   e. **Teams only**—Use this setting if you want your users to use only Teams. Note that even with this setting, users can still join meetings hosted in Skype for Business.

4. Select **Save**.

To set the coexistence mode for a specific user, follow these steps:

1. Log on to the TAC at *https://admin.teams.microsoft.com.*

2. In the left menu, select **Users**.

3. Select the user or users you wish to change, and then select **Edit settings.**

4. Scroll down to the **Teams upgrade** section.

5. In the drop-down list under **Coexistence mode**, select the desired mode.

6. Set **Notify the Skype for Business user** to **On** if desired.

7. Set **Migrate this user's meetings to Teams** to **On** if desired. If set to **On**, this option will use the MMS to migrate meetings, as discussed in the previous section. (Remember the caveats for the MMS.)

Use Teams Advisor to assess and identify steps to roll out Microsoft Teams

Microsoft Teams Advisor, also known as the Advisor for Teams, is a guided walkthrough for rolling out Microsoft Teams and is included in the TAC. Teams Advisor can be used first to assess your Microsoft 365 tenant configuration to ensure that it is set up optimally for Teams, and it will provide guidance for any necessary changes. It then creates a deployment team within your Microsoft Teams tenant that includes a Planner plan for all the tasks needed to successfully roll out Teams. All you as the Teams admin will need to do is identify the actual coworkers who will be a part of the deployment team, add them to the Deployment Team, and assign them to the tasks that were created in the Planner plan. This is a great way to quickly determine what needs to be done and what specific tasks are required for deployment.

To use Teams Advisor, do the following:

1. Log on to the TAC at *https://admin.teams.microsoft.com*.

2. In the left menu, select **Planning**.

3. Select **Teams Advisor**. You should see three Teams workloads with details, as shown in Figure 1-4.

FIGURE 1-4 Deploying Teams Advisor

4. You can choose to view the assessments for any of the workloads, and you may see that some are already complete. Select a workload and then select **View** on the right side.

5. Scroll through to see the associated tasks. Start with the **Project kickoff** by selecting **View details**. You will see a description, a progress section, and a checklist of tasks that need to be done.

6. At the bottom of the screen, select **Next.**

7. Add the team members you will be working with to deploy Teams, then select **Apply**.

8. When you have finished adding team members, select **Create**.

9. Teams will create the deployment team and channels, and populate Planner with the relevant tasks. You can track this in the TAC, as shown in Figure 1-5.

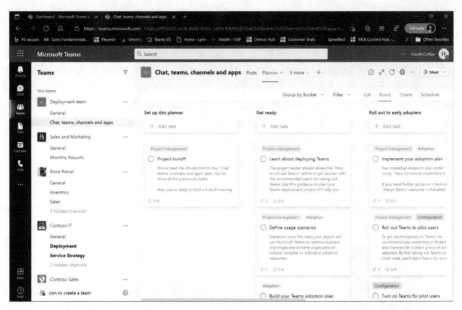

FIGURE 1-5 The "Chat, teams, channels and apps" channel in the deployment team with the tasks added to Planner

You can read more about using Microsoft Teams Advisor at *https://docs.microsoft.com/ en-us/microsoftteams/use-advisor-teams-roll-out*.

Skill 1.2: Plan and configure network settings for Microsoft Teams

Microsoft Teams' networking requirements are fairly straightforward, but a customer's experience with Teams can be greatly impacted when these requirements are not met. Teams is often referred to as the "canary in the coal mine" when it comes to the network. If you are not familiar with the phrase, it refers to a time when toxic gases could build up in coal mines and present a risk to the miners. Canaries, being more susceptible to these toxic gases, were kept in cages in the same area as the miners. If they began to show signs of distress, it was a clear indication that the air was becoming unsafe, and the miners would need to evacuate. Teams is susceptible to poor network conditions, so it can be the first application to show issues if a network is unhealthy. Teams' reporting and diagnostics are also dependent on network information, and the requirements for emergency calling (e911) are also very dependent on network information.

In this skill section, we focus on all things networking related to Microsoft Teams.

This skill covers how to:

- Plan for successful network deployment by using Network Planner
- Calculate network bandwidth capacity for Microsoft Teams voice, video, meetings, and live events
- Assess network readiness by using Network Testing Companion
- Configure network ports and protocols used by the Microsoft Teams client application
- Configure media optimizations by using QoS

Plan for successful network deployment by using Network Planner

Network Planner is a tool that helps Teams administrators to determine and organize their network requirements. By entering specifics about your locations' network connectivity and needs, you can calculate bandwidth requirements for deploying Teams in each of your locations.

The planner includes three recommended personas for Teams, including office workers, remote workers, and Teams room systems. One assumption for the three included personas is that each will use all the functions within Teams. You can create up to three additional custom personas if the Microsoft-recommended ones do not match your users and you want to calculate based on users having only a limited subset of Teams features available to them. To use Network Planner, do the following.

Create a custom persona (optional)

If you want to create a custom persona, follow these steps:

1. Log on to the TAC at *https://admin.teams.microsoft.com*.
2. In the left menu, select **Planning**.
3. Select **Network planner**.
4. Select the **Personas** tab, then select **+Custom persona.**
5. Enter the name and a description.
6. Select the features that the persona will use (called permissions in this wizard).

7. Select **Apply**, as shown in Figure 1-6.

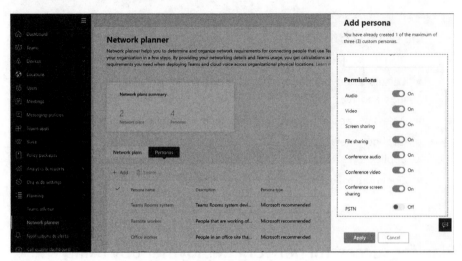

FIGURE 1-6 Creating a custom persona in Network Planner

Build your plan

You are now ready to build a network plan:

1. If necessary, select the **Network plans** tab.

2. Select **+Add** to create a new network plan.

3. Enter a name and a description for this plan. It's good to be short but intuitive with your naming.

4. Select the plan name.

5. Add sites that correspond to your network locations. You will need to add a name and a description, the physical address, the number of users, any subnets associated with that location, whether or not the site is WAN-enabled (and, if it is, the WAN capacity), whether or not it has local internet egress, and what, if any, PSTN egress it has. When you are creating sites, anywhere a WAN link or an internet egress link exists and all user traffic between a client and the Microsoft Teams service would be dependent on that link being a location.

6. Select **Save** when done, as shown in Figure 1-7.

FIGURE 1-7 Creating a site in Network planner

Create a report

Once you have all the sites created, you can create a report:

1. Select the **Reports** tab.

2. Select **Start a report**.

3. Enter a name and a description.

You will see the number of users you entered for each site automatically distributed among personas. Review and update as necessary, including adding your custom personas if desired. You will need to allocate all users before you can continue, as shown in Figure 1-8.

FIGURE 1-8 Generating a report in Network Planner

4. Select **Generate report**.

On the next screen, you will see the projected impact from Microsoft Teams. You can change the view and export the chart to PDF if desired, as shown in Figure 1-9.

Network site	Type	Impact	Audio	Video	Screenshare	Office 365 server tr...	PSTN
CLT1	WAN	3.117 Mbps	0.101 Mbps	2.258 Mbps	0.758 Mbps	0 Mbps	0 Mbps
150 network users	Office 365	13.8797 Mbps	0.5022 Mbps	9.606 Mbps	3.52 Mbps	0.2515 Mbps	0 Mbps

FIGURE 1-9 The projected impact to the CLT1 site

Reports are saved and can be edited and run again if your personas, assumptions, or other data changes.

EXAM TIP

Network Planner can be accessed by Global Admins, Teams administrators, and Teams Communications Administrators. No other roles have access to Network Planner.

Calculate network bandwidth capacity for Microsoft Teams voice, video, meetings, and live events

Ensuring that you have enough available bandwidth for Microsoft Teams requires that you have a good idea of what your users will be using throughout the day. Microsoft Teams will optimize media quality based on what bandwidth is available to the client, and it will give priority to audio over video when there is not enough bandwidth to provide optimum quality to both. Teams uses an efficient codec to encode both audio and video. The actual bandwidth used for any specific scenario may vary based on a number of factors, including video resolution and how much data is changing from one sample to the next. Teams will also automatically scale up to consume more bandwidth when it is available to provide the best quality and will scale down when available bandwidth is less. Table 1-3 provides average bandwidth usage for most scenarios, per user.

TABLE 1-3 Microsoft Teams client average bandwidth by scenario, per user

Bandwidth	Scenario
30 Kbps	1:1 audio calling
130 Kbps	1:1 audio calling with screen sharing

Bandwidth	Scenario
500 Kbps	1:1 video calling (360p at 30 fps)
1.2 Mbps	1:1 video calling (720p at 30 fps)
1.5 Mbps	1:1 video calling (1080p at 30 fps)
500 Kbps up/1 Mbps down	Group video calling (360p at 30 fps)
1 Mbps up/2 Mbps down	Group video calling (540p at 30 fps)

When planning Teams live events, consider if you will have a large number of users in the same location, using the same WAN/internet egress. Teams live events use adaptive bitrate streaming (ABR) to reduce bandwidth requirements, but the stream is unicast only. If you have a large number of users in the same location all attending the same Teams live event, the aggregate bandwidth to view the event may impact your network egress. Teams live events can use third-party software-defined network (SDN) or enterprise content delivery network (eCDN) solutions for distribution. There are several third-party SDN/eCDN solutions for use on your network to reduce impact from large Teams live events with many attendees in the same location. See *https://docs.microsoft.com/en-us/microsoftteams/teams-live-events/set-up-for-teams-live-events#step-4-set-up-a-video-distribution-solution-for-live-events-in-teams* for information on these providers.

Assess network readiness by using Network Testing Companion

The Skype for Business and Microsoft Teams Network Testing Companion is a graphical tool that can help you validate media quality from a client endpoint to the Microsoft Teams service's media edge endpoints. You can download it from the PowerShell Gallery by installing the module on to your workstation. To do this, follow these steps:

1. Open an administrative PowerShell session.
2. Run the cmdlet `Install-Module -Name NetworkTestingCompanion`.
3. If you are prompted to trust the repository, enter **Y**.
4. Once installed, you can create a shortcut on your desktop by running the command `Invoke-ToolCreateShortcuts` and pressing Enter. Or you can directly launch the tool from the PowerShell session by running the command `Invoke-NetworkTestingClient` and pressing Enter.

Network Testing Companion will check for updates and then launch a GUI, as shown in Figure 1-10.

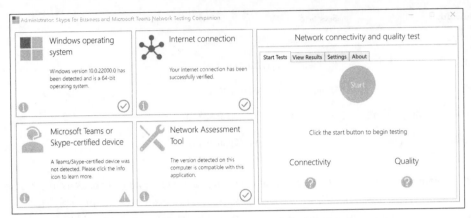

FIGURE 1-10 The Skype for Business and Microsoft Teams Network Testing Companion

5. Select the green **Start** button to begin the tests. The connectivity test will run first, followed by the quality test. By default, each test runs for one iteration and will take a moment to complete. If you want to run more, you can select the **Settings** tab and adjust things there.

6. When the tests are complete, you can view the results. Ideally, you will see green check boxes that show everything is within tolerances and that all endpoints are accessible across all ports, as shown in Figure 1-11.

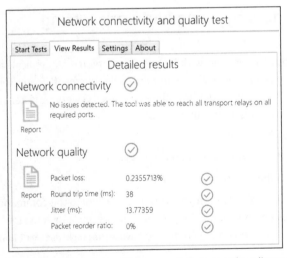

FIGURE 1-11 The results of the connectivity test and quality tests

7. If you want more details, you can select the Report icon next to each report to open it in your default text editor.

If any of the values fail, you will need to investigate the cause. It could be a firewall or proxy issue if the connectivity report indicates an endpoint cannot be reached on both TCP 443 and UDP 3478. If the network quality report indicates a failing value, you may need to engage your network team to determine where the problem exists. The issue could be with an overloaded wireless access point, or an overutilized network egress point, or even bad routing. The specific values will not always immediately indicate where a problem is, but they will confirm a problem exists and help you narrow down where to investigate.

Configure network ports and protocols used by the Microsoft Teams client application

Microsoft Teams has very straightforward networking requirements. When a network is healthy and well configured, and has an optimal connection to Office 365, Teams works very well. But when any issues with the network issue, they can manifest as poor performance. Network Testing Companion is a useful tool for evaluating network performance issues on a per-client basis, but you should start out by ensuring your network is configured properly for consuming all Microsoft 365 services, especially Teams.

You should review and follow the recommendations documented by Microsoft at *https://aka.ms/pnc* to get the best results. The following guidelines are a summary:

- Ensure users have the most direct route to the internet.

- Ensure that DNS resolution happens along that same direct route to the internet. You want your users' traffic to egress your network, and to ingress to Microsoft's network, as quickly as possible. Keeping DNS resolution local to your users not only improves name resolution performance, but also helps direct users' traffic to the closest Microsoft endpoints.

- Do not attempt to proxy Microsoft Teams traffic or force it through a VPN for remote users. Split tunneling for VPN access is the right way to go.

- Ensure that both TCP and UDP ports are open from your clients to the Microsoft IP address ranges directly. Streaming traffic (audio, video, and screen sharing) should be able to use UDP to reduce latency. You should not have to permit *any* unsolicited inbound traffic. This is outbound only.

In addition to the bandwidth requirements discussed previously, you should ensure that the required connectivity is in place. Microsoft maintains documentation on the required Microsoft 365 endpoints at *https://docs.microsoft.com/en-us/microsoft-365/enterprise/urls-and-ip-address-ranges?view=o365-worldwide*. As new endpoints and services are added, this documentation is updated, so it's important to make sure your permitted connectivity is current. You can subscribe to an RSS feed on that page if you wish. To fully use Microsoft Teams, you should follow all the guidance on that page and ensure that clients have access to all required and optional endpoints. The most important things to pay attention to, ensuring direct connectivity, without proxying or routing through VPN before going out to the service, are detailed in Table 1-4.

TABLE 1-4 Microsoft Teams connectivity requirements

Category	Addresses	Protocol	Ports
Optimize Required	13.107.64.0/18, 52.112.0.0/14, 52.120.0.0/14	UDP	3478–3481
Allow Required	*.lync.com, *.teams.microsoft.com, teams.microsoft.com 13.107.64.0/18, 52.112.0.0/14, 52.120.0.0/14, 52.238.119.141/32, 52.244.160.207/32, 2603:1027::/48, 2603:1037::/48, 2603:1047::/48, 2603:1057::/48, 2620:1ec:6::/48, 2620:1ec:40::/42	TCP	80, 443
Allow Required	*.broadcast.skype.com, broadcast.skype.com 13.107.64.0/18, 52.112.0.0/14, 52.120.0.0/14, 52.238.119.141/32, 52.244.160.207/32, 2603:1027::/48, 2603:1037::/48, 2603:1047::/48, 2603:1057::/48, 2620:1ec:6::/48, 2620:1ec:40::/42	TCP	443
Default Required	*.sfbassets.com	TCP	80, 443
Default Required	*.keydelivery.mediaservices.windows.net, *.msecnd.net, *.streaming.mediaservices.windows.net, ajax.aspnetcdn. com, mlccdn.blob.core.windows.net	TCP	80, 443
Default Required	aka.ms, amp.azure.net	TCP	80, 443
Default Optional Notes: Federation with Skype and public IM connectivity: Contact picture retrieval	*.users.storage.live.com	TCP	80, 443
Default Optional Notes: Applies only to those who deploy the Conference Room Systems	*.adl.windows.com	TCP	80, 443
Allow Optional Notes: Teams: Messaging interop with Skype for Business	*.skypeforbusiness.com 13.107.64.0/18, 52.112.0.0/14, 52.120.0.0/14, 52.238.119.141/32, 52.244.160.207/32, 2603:1027::/48, 2603:1037::/48, 2603:1047::/48, 2603:1057::/48, 2620:1ec:6::/48, 2620:1ec:40::/42	TCP	80, 443
Default Required	*.msedge.net, compass-ssl.microsoft.com	TCP	80, 443
Default Required	*.mstea.ms, *.secure.skypeassets.com, mlccdnprod.azureedge.net, videoplayercdn.osi.office.net	TCP	80, 443

Category	Addresses	Protocol	Ports
Default Optional Notes: Yammer third-party integration	*.tenor.com	TCP	80, 443
Default Required	*.skype.com	TCP	80, 443

Optimize means to permit direct connectivity without proxy or unnecessary routing through a VPN. The Allow *should* do the same but is more tolerant of latency and could be proxied and/or routed through VPN if you must. Default means that you can treat it just like any other default traffic, proxying and/or routing through VPN if that is your default. Remember also that the entries in Table 1-4 do not include the required connectivity for authentication to Microsoft 365, or for using other services, including Exchange Online, SharePoint Online, and OneDrive for Business. Refer to *https://docs.microsoft.com/en-us/microsoft-365/enterprise/urls-and-ip-address-ranges* for the full documentation on Microsoft 365 connectivity requirements.

Configure media optimizations by using QoS

Quality of service (QoS) is a method for tagging certain traffic to provide priority access across a network. When a network is heavily congested, traffic that is tagged for higher-priority access using Differentiated Services Code Point (DSCP) values is given precedence through routers, helping to minimize the latency and maximize the performance of that traffic. On a LAN or WAN, if all the network devices support it, QoS works very well to prioritize real-time traffic such as the streaming traffic Microsoft Teams uses. However, QoS tags are not honored on the internet, so it's important to get your traffic from your edge to Microsoft's edge as optimally as possible. Microsoft peers with hundreds of ISPs in thousands of locations, so if your DNS and internet egress are optimized, latency over the internet should not be a concern. It's on your busy LAN/WAN that QoS can help.

This may seem counterintuitive to some, so look at it like this. The internet connection to Microsoft 365 is one of the largest sets of internet circuits in the world. Bandwidth is simply not a problem between ISPs and Microsoft's datacenters. Think of it as the interstate, without any of the construction that might slow things down where you drive. Your local area network and wide area network are the series of local and secondary roads that your network traffic has to take to get to the interstate. QoS lets certain traffic take the reserved or express or HOV lanes so that it gets to move in front of normal traffic. If you are using QoS to mark Teams traffic, that means it gets from the client endpoint to the interstate with priority access across your network. Once it's off your network, QoS doesn't do anything anymore, but at that point the "roads" are no longer congested so it's no longer needed.

If all of your network equipment supports QoS, then you can use it, if you need it, on your network. Don't assume that you do. though. Modern, well-designed networks seldom see the kinds of latency and congestion that older networks did, and you may not have any network issues that QoS could overcome. But if you see performance issues, and you validate with network monitoring tools and/or Teams Network Testing Companion that there is jitter, packet loss, and/or excessive round-trip time (RTT) between your endpoint and Microsoft's datacenters, implementing QoS may help. This does assume, though, that all other aspects of your connection have already been optimized, including ensuring all endpoints are directly accessible across both the TCP and UDP ports; you are not trying to proxy Teams traffic; you are not routing remote users' Teams traffic over the VPN; and your DNS resolution and internet egress are both optimal. If you are forcing traffic to route halfway across the continent, or across the ocean, to get to an egress point, or if your DNS resolution is chained so that queries to the internet all originate from the main location but your remote locations are in other regions, then you need to fix that. QoS is not going to help you in those situations.

You can implement QoS in two different ways. The first is to use your network hardware (routers, firewalls, etc.) to implement QoS based on network traffic, examining the ports and network addresses to assign QoS. This approach is preferred since it is able to apply QoS to Teams traffic whether it is coming from a client or from the service, and it ensures that all clients' traffic is prioritized. Use the network connectivity requirements discussed previously to identity the ports and network addresses to tag, and follow your specific hardware vendor's directions on how to implement this. This may need to be handled by your network team if you do not have the necessary access to do this.

The other way is to use Group Policy (GPO) to configure Windows clients to tag Teams traffic at the endpoint. This approach still requires that all network devices support QoS, but it lets you configure the Windows clients rather than making changes on network devices. Of course, this will not cover Mac, Linux, iOS, or Android clients, or any Windows clients that are not domain joined, which is why doing this on the network infrastructure is preferable.

Whether configuring network hardware or using GPO, the settings in Table 1-5 are recommended as a starting point.

TABLE 1-5 Recommended DSCP settings for using QoS with Microsoft Teams

Media traffic type	Client source port range	Protocol	DSCP value	DSCP class
Audio	50000–50019	TCP and UDP	46	Expedited Forwarding (EF)
Video	50020–50039	TCP and UDP	34	Assured Forwarding (AF41)
Application or screen sharing	50040–50059	TCP and UDP	18	Assured Forwarding (AF21)

> ***NEED MORE REVIEW?*** **GOING DEEPER ON QOS**
>
> See *https://docs.microsoft.com/en-us/microsoftteams/qos-in-teams* for more information on using QoS with Teams, and see *https://docs.microsoft.com/en-us/microsoftteams/qos-in-teams-clients* to learn how to implement QoS using GPO.

Skill 1.3: Implement governance and lifecycle management for Microsoft Teams

In this skill section we will cover governance and lifecycle management in Teams. These practices can help with the overall ownership and administration of Microsoft Teams, ensure consistent naming, and ensure that legacy Teams have a lifecycle that keeps things clean when a Team is no longer required. If you have ever tried to figure out the last time someone used an email distribution list or an old SharePoint site, you will appreciate setting this up at the start.

This skill covers how to:

- Create and manage team templates
- Set up policies for Microsoft 365 group creation
- Configure Microsoft 365 groups, expiration policy, and naming policy
- Archive, unarchive, delete, and restore a team
- Configure and manage update policies

Create and manage team templates

Templates enable you to quickly create new teams for common purposes; configure new teams with a consistent set of channels, tabs, and apps; or "clone" existing teams if you wish to reuse their setup for other teams. Doing so can save time when you're configuring multiple teams and also ensures that users have a consistent experience across the many teams they may create or join. Whether you create your own templates from scratch, use an existing one as is, or duplicate an existing one to customize for your organization, templates are a great way to quickly and consistently roll out new teams, ensuring that the users will have what they need to be productive immediately.

Teams admins manage templates in the TAC, and Teams users can then use templates in the Teams client to create new teams. To manage templates, as a Teams admin, do the following:

1. Log on to the TAC at *https://admin.teams.microsoft.com*.

2. In the left menu, expand **Teams**, and select **Team templates**.

You will see several templates that come with Teams automatically, as shown in Figure 1-12.

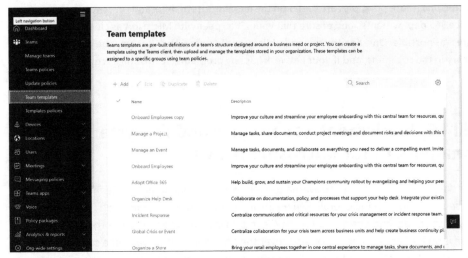

FIGURE 1-12 Teams templates in the TAC

3. You can add new templates, edit existing templates that you have created or copied, duplicate a template, or delete a template that you have created. The included templates cannot be edited or deleted, but they can be hidden if you don't want users to use them.

4. To add a new template, select **Add**.

5. When adding, you can create a new template from scratch, use an existing team as a template, or start with an existing template, as shown in Figure 1-13.

FIGURE 1-13 Creating a new template

6. For this walkthrough, choose **Start with an existing template** and then select **Next**.

7. Select the box next to **Onboard Employees** and then select **Next**.

8. Give your template a unique, descriptive name; enter descriptive information; and change the locale if necessary. Then select **Next**.

9. On this screen, you can begin your customizations. You can add (or remove) channels, add (or remove) tabs in channels, determine whether they show by default, and add (or remove) apps. Make your desired changes, and then select **Submit**.

10. Now that you have a custom template, you may want to hide the original. In the left menu, select **Templates policies**.

11. Select **Global (Org-wide default)** and select **Edit**.

12. Select the original template, and select **Hide**.

You can also create additional template policies if you want some users to be able to use some templates but hide them from others.

1. In the **Template policies** section, create a new policy and name it appropriately.

2. Select the policy, and then select **Manage users**.

3. Add the users to which you wish the new template policy to apply.

REAL WORLD   **ALWAYS DUPLICATE, NEVER JUST EDIT**

You cannot edit the default templates using the user interface. You can copy any of them and then edit the copy. That way, if you make a mistake or just want to go back to the original, you still have that original template to start from, rather than having to remember and reverse every change you made. If you do make copies and customize them for your organization, use template policies to hide your originals so that only your modified duplicates show. That way, your users can pick only from the modified templates you have created.

Set up policies for Microsoft 365 group creation

Microsoft 365 groups are one of the core components of many Microsoft 365 services, including the following:

- Outlook
- SharePoint
- Yammer
- Stream
- Planner
- PowerBI
- Project
- And, of course, Teams

By default, all users can create Microsoft 365 groups, which is necessary to support all users being able to create a new team in Microsoft Teams. As teamwork does not always involve IT, creating teams should typically not need to involve IT, either. But if your organization does want to limit regular users creating Microsoft 365 groups and require them to go through IT in order to create a new team (or anything else that uses a Microsoft 365 group), then you can limit this. But please note that doing so is not necessary to achieve a consistent naming, or to force expiration, which we will cover in the next section.

To set up policies for Microsoft 365 group creation, you need to create a Microsoft 365 group, assign permissions to that group, and then add users who you want to permit to create other groups into that first group. Then you need to download and run a PowerShell (PS) script to update Azure AD to permit this new group and deny any other nonadministrative users. *See https://docs.microsoft.com/en-us/microsoft-365/solutions/manage-creation-of-groups?view=o365-worldwide* for specific steps, as well as the PS script to accomplish this.

REAL WORLD   **THERE ARE EXCEPTIONS AS WELL AS LICENSING REQUIREMENTS**

You cannot restrict certain roles from being able to create Microsoft 365 groups. Admin roles will always be able to create groups through the Microsoft 365 portals relevant to their role, and/or through PowerShell. Also, note that if you want to limit Microsoft 365 group creation, you will need Azure AD Premium Plan 1 licenses for every user who configures restrictions as well as every nonadministrative user you do actually want to permit to create Microsoft 365 groups.

Configure Microsoft 365 groups, expiration policy, and naming policy

Microsoft 365 groups are an Azure Active Directory (AAD) construct and so are configured and managed primarily in the Azure Active Directory portal or through AAD PowerShell commands. Using either, you can manage any groups over which you have administrative rights. To manage a group using the AAD portal, follow these steps:

1. Log on to the Azure portal at *https://portal.azure.com*.

2. In the **Search resources** box at the top, type **Groups** and then select **Groups** in the results.

3. In the **Groups** blade, you will see all the groups in your Azure AD. You can search for a specific group, or filter to only see Microsoft 365 groups if desired. Groups associated with Microsoft Teams are group type Microsoft 365. Find the group you want to manage and select it in the portal, as shown in Figure 1-14.

FIGURE 1-14 Managing Office 365 Groups in the Azure portal

Organizations large and small may see a proliferation of teams, and the corresponding Microsoft 365 groups, as users spin up new teams and then stop using them when the specific need has passed. Setting an expiration policy enables an organization to more easily clean up groups that are no longer needed, and as a result also clean up stale teams, SharePoint sites, and Outlook groups. By default, expiration of Microsoft 365 Groups is turned off, but Global Admins can enable this for their organization if desired.

Expiration can be set for 180 days, 365 days, or a custom value greater than 30 days. As a group approaches expiration, notifications are sent out to the owners of a group, notifying them that they need to renew a group at 30, 15, and 1 day before expiration. If they take no action, the group is deleted. Groups that are deleted are *soft deleted*, meaning an admin can restore the group for up to 30 days after the deletion. Note that if a group has no owner, notifications will default to an email contact that is required. Also note that if a group is subject to a retention policy, deleting an expired group will not result in lost data; retention will maintain it.

To set an expiration policy, do the following:

1. Log on to the Azure portal at *https://portal.azure.com*.

2. In the **Search resources** box at the top, type **Groups** and then select **Groups** in the results.

3. In the left menu, select **Expiration**.

4. Choose the group lifetime you wish to enforce. Remember that the minimum custom value is 30 days.

5. Enter an administrative email contact, which will be notified for groups that have no current owner (such as when a group owner has since left the company).

6. Enable the expiration for All, Selected, or None. If you choose Selected, you can select up to 500 groups. Note also that an organization can have only one group expiration policy. In Figure 1-15, we are setting a two-year expiration policy for all groups.

FIGURE 1-15 Setting a Groups Expiration policy

7. Select **Save** when done.

EXAM TIP

Expiration will be calculated from the date the group was created, not when the policy was created.

NOTE   OFFICE 365 GROUPS MAY AUTOMATICALLY RENEW

The following actions will automatically renew a group, resetting the clock on when the next time expiration will come up.

- SharePoint—Any user views, edits, downloads, moves, shares, or uploads a file.
- Outlook—Any user joins, reads/writes a message, or likes a message.
- Microsoft Teams—any user visits a Teams channel.

Finally, you may wish to enforce a Microsoft 365 Group naming policy. You can upload a list of up to 5,000 terms that cannot be a part of a Microsoft 365 Group name, and you can also set a specific prefix or suffix to every group name. This too is done through the Azure Active Directory management portal.

1. Log on to the Azure portal at *https://portal.azure.com*.

2. In the **Search resources** box at the top, type **Groups** and then select **Groups** in the results.

3. In the left menu, select **Naming policy**.

4. If you need to prevent certain words from being used, select the **Blocked words** tab, create a CSV file containing up to 5,000 words, and upload it.

   If you want to enforce a prefix, suffix, or both, select the **Group naming policy** tab and select either or both **Add prefix** and **Add suffix**. When enforcing prefixes and suffixes, you can use specific strings, or Azure AD attributes. In the example shown in Figure 1-16, the company name will begin every group name, followed by a hyphen, and then a suffix will be added that notes the department.

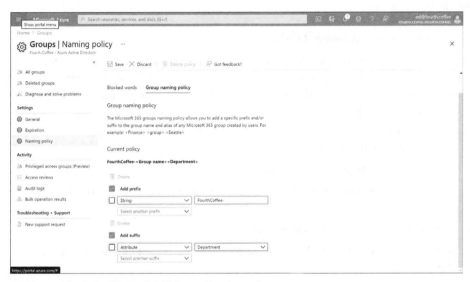

FIGURE 1-16 Setting a Microsoft 365 Group Naming policy

Archive, unarchive, delete, and restore a team

You may also want to archive a team if it is no longer active, without deleting it. Later, you may wish to unarchive it so that it can be actively used again. And of course, you may want to delete a team, which could lead to the need to restore a team. All of these functions are handled in the TAC (or via PowerShell). To do this in the TAC:

1. Log on to the TAC at *https://admin.teams.microsoft.com*.

2. In the left menu, expand **Teams**, and then select **Manage teams**.

3. Select the team or teams you wish to manage.

4. To archive a team, select the **Archive** button.

   You will be prompted to "Make the SharePoint site read-only for team members," which is recommended if you are archiving the team, as shown in Figure 1-17.

Archive ✕

This will freeze all of the team activity, but you and team owners will still be able to add or remove members and update roles. You can unarchive the team anytime.

☑ Make the SharePoint site read-only for team members

[Archive] [Cancel]

FIGURE 1-17 Archiving a team

5. Select the option, and select **Archive**.

To unarchive a team, simply pick the team or teams, which are archived, and select the button to unarchive. The process to delete a team is the same. Simply select the team or teams you wish to delete, and then select the Delete button. Undeleting a team requires a little more, though. Remember that there is a direct relationship between a Microsoft 365 Group and a Microsoft Team. When you delete a team, you delete the Microsoft 365 Group. To restore the team, you must restore the group:

1. Log on to the Azure portal at *https://portal.azure.com*.

2. In the **Search resources** box at the top, type **Groups** and then select **Groups** in the results.

3. In the left menu, select **Deleted groups**.

4. Select the group or groups you wish to restore, and then select **Restore group**, as shown in Figure 1-18.

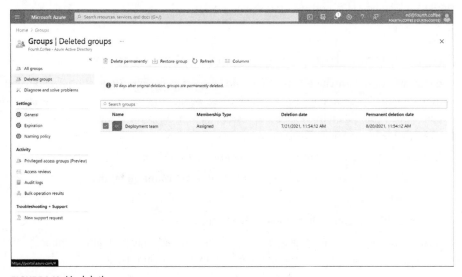

FIGURE 1-18 Undeleting a group

5. Return to the TAC to view the restored team. You may need to refresh or move to a different pane and then back again to see the restored team in the list of teams.

EXAM TIP

Remember that you only have 30 days to restore a group after it was deleted. After 30 days, the group is permanently deleted.

Configure and manage update policies

Teams update policies manage Teams and Office preview users to control what features users may see in pre-release or preview when using Microsoft Teams. The Global (Org-wide default) policy controls the experience for all users. If you want all to have the same experience, use this policy. But if you want to have a set of users get a new feature earlier so that you can evaluate it or update your user training, you can create one or more custom policies for your users.

To configure and manage update policies, do the following:

1. Log on to the TAC at *https://admin.teams.microsoft.com*.
2. In the left menu, expand **Teams** and then select **Update policies**.
3. Note the Global (Org-wide default policy). If you want the entire org to receive updates early, edit that policy and set **Show preview features** to **On**.
4. Select **Apply** to finish.
5. If instead you want to target a subset of users, select **+Add** to create a new policy, and set **Show preview features** to **On**.
6. Select **Apply** to finish.
7. If you want to manage individual users (a small number), select the check box next to your new policy, and then select **Manage users**. Search for, and add, the users you want to apply this to.
8. If instead you want to apply to a group, go to the **Group policy assignment** tab in the **Policy packages** pane.
9. Search for the group you wish to use, and select the policy package you created earlier. Note that it may take several minutes for the new package to appear in this list.

Skill 1.4: Configure and manage guest access

One of the most useful aspects of Microsoft Teams is how it enables organizations to collaborate with others outside of the organization, whether those are partners, vendors, consultants, suppliers, or even customers. Securely managing guest access is a critical part of managing Microsoft Teams so that your users can safely and securely collaborate with others, while ensuring that you protect information that should be private.

This skill covers how to:

- Configure guest users for Microsoft Teams
- Configure guest permissions for a team
- Configure meeting and live events experiences for guests
- Configure messaging and calling options for guests
- Remove guests
- Manage Azure AD access review for guests
- Configure guest access from Azure AD portal

Configure guest users for Microsoft Teams

Guest access in Microsoft Teams is dependent on settings in several areas. From the top of the hierarchy down, this includes Azure Active Directory, Microsoft 365, SharePoint, and then finally Teams.

Azure Active Directory external collaboration settings

External sharing first needs to be enabled in the External collaboration settings in Azure Active Directory. To set/confirm this, follow these steps:

1. Log on to the Azure portal at *https://portal.azure.com*.
2. In the **Search resources** box at the top, type **External Identities** and press Enter.
3. In the left menu, select **External collaboration settings**.

   Review the settings as shown in Figure 1-19. Make any adjustments as necessary.

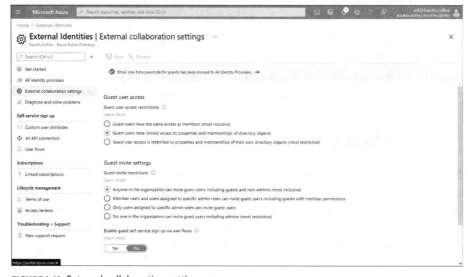

FIGURE 1-19 External collaboration settings

Microsoft 365 Groups guest settings

Since access to Teams is governed by Microsoft 365 Groups, you next want to ensure that your Microsoft 365 Group settings permit guests.

1. Log on to the Microsoft 365 Admin Center at *https://admin.microsoft.com*.

2. In the left menu, select **Show all**, and then expand **Settings**, expand **Org settings**, and select the **Services** tab.

3. Select **Microsoft 365 Groups.**

4. Ensure that both "Let group owners add people outside..." and "Let guest group members access group content" are selected, as shown in Figure 1-20.

FIGURE 1-20 Microsoft 365 Groups external settings

SharePoint organization-level sharing settings

Next, you want to review the SharePoint external sharing settings:

1. From the Microsoft 365 admin portal, in the left menu, scroll down to **Admin centers** and launch the **SharePoint admin console**.

2. Expand **Policies**, and then select **Sharing**.

Review and adjust (if necessary) the **External sharing** settings for both SharePoint and OneDrive for Business, as shown in Figure 1-21.

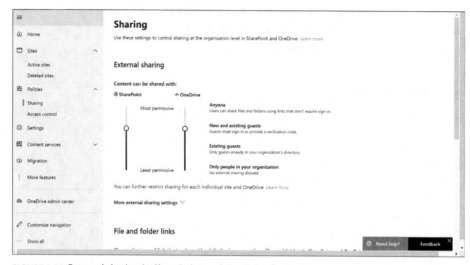

FIGURE 1-21 External sharing in SharePoint and OneDrive for Business

3. Once a team has been created, you may adjust the permissions on the team's individual SharePoint site, if necessary. Expand **Sites**, select **Active sites**, and then select the site that corresponds to the team.

4. Select the **Policies** tab; then under **External sharing**, select **Edit**.

5. You can set site-specific permissions for this team's site if necessary. You can also reset the site to use the organization-level settings by selecting the link at the very bottom of this pane, as shown in Figure 1-22.

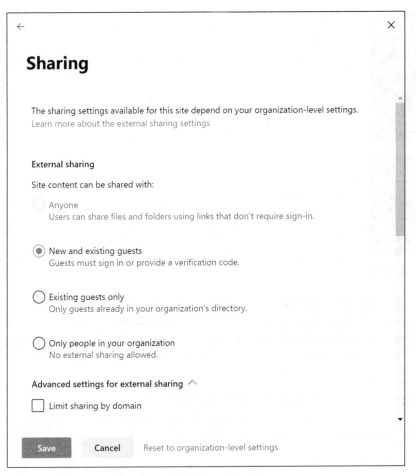

FIGURE 1-22 Sharing settings for a specific SharePoint site

Microsoft Teams guest settings

Finally, you can configure guest access specific to Microsoft Teams. Teams guest access is on by default for new tenants created after February 2021 but was off by default for tenants created prior to February 2021. This access is dependent on the settings in Azure AD, Microsoft 365, and SharePoint, so make sure you have verified/configured those first. Then, to check to see if guest access is on (or not,) do the following:

1. Log on to the TAC at *https://admin.teams.microsoft.com*.

2. In the left menu, expand **Org-wide Settings**, and select **Guest Access**.

You will see the status at the top of this page, and you can make changes if necessary, as shown in Figure 1-23.

FIGURE 1-23 Guest access

3. Once Guest Access is turned on, you can control what can be shared with or accessed by guests in Microsoft Teams on this page. Note that this controls what guests can do **once they have explicitly been added as a guest to a team**, but does not give any guest access on its own. By default, all capabilities are enabled when guest access is permitted.

> **NEED MORE REVIEW? COLLABORATING AS A TEAM**
>
> For more information on guest access, see *https://docs.microsoft.com/en-us/microsoft-365/solutions/collaborate-as-team?view=o365-worldwide.*

Configure guest permissions for a team

With Microsoft Teams now able to support guest access, you can work on setting specific guest permission for each team that requires guests. By default, each team user (or admin) you create will inherit the Guest Access settings from the Org-wide settings, but a team owner can configure specific settings on individual teams if necessary using the Microsoft Teams client or the web client. Here are the steps:

1. As a team owner, access the properties of your team in the client by selecting the ellipsis (...) next to the team name.

2. From the drop-down list, select **Manage team**.

3. Select the **Settings** tab.

4. Select **Guest permissions**.

5. Adjust **Guest permissions** as desired, as shown in Figure 1-24.

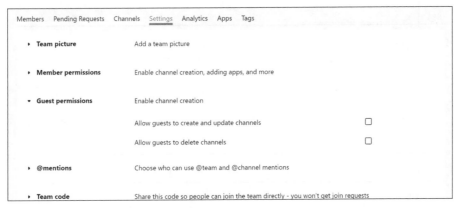

FIGURE 1-24 Guest permissions for an individual team

Configure meeting and live events experiences for guests

People outside the organization can be invited to both Teams meetings and Teams live events without being added to a team or allowing guest access to Teams. Settings that control guest experiences for both are administered in the TAC, and organizations can set up multiple policies if required for meetings and live events scheduled by different users. To configure meeting and live events experiences for guests, do the following:

1. Log on to the TAC at *https://admin.teams.microsoft.com*.

2. In the left menu, expand **Meetings**, and then select **Meeting policies**.

3. There are several included policies, or you can create a new one. For this, select the **Global (Org-wide default)** policy, which will apply to all users who don't explicitly have a different policy applied.

4. Scroll down to **Participants & guests**.

5. Adjust settings if necessary. The defaults are shown in Figure 1-25.

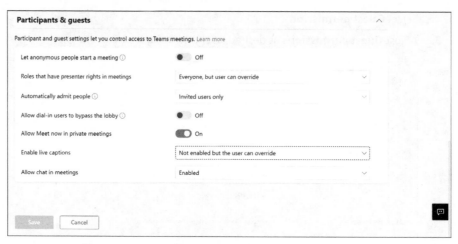

FIGURE 1-25 Participants & Guests settings for meetings

To configure settings for Teams live events, do the following:

1. Select **Live events policies**.

2. Again, you can have multiple policies here. The **Global (Org-wide default)** will apply to Teams live events scheduled by anyone who does not have another policy applied to them. Select it to edit.

3. Adjust if necessary. The defaults are shown in Figure 1-26.

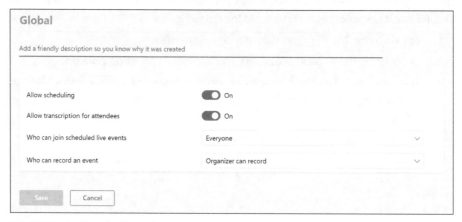

FIGURE 1-26 Settings for Teams live events

Configure messaging and calling options for guests

Guest messaging and calling options have to do with external federation using SIP, but not PSTN calling. This external access is often referred to as federation, and it controls whether or not your users can make and receive VoIP calls and chat with external users. External access is controlled in Org-wide settings, and can be turned off or on, and it can be configured explicitly to either allow or block specific SIP domains. You also have the option to allow or block communication with users of the Skype consumer service. To configure messaging and calling options for guests, follow these steps:

1. Log on to the TAC at *https://admin.teams.microsoft.com*.

2. In the left menu, scroll down to **Org-wide settings**, and select **External access**.

3. To permit external access, turn on both settings as shown in Figure 1-27.

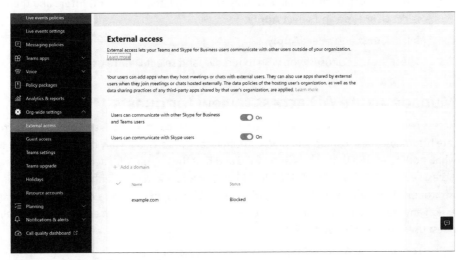

FIGURE 1-27 Settings for External access

4. If you want to block a specific domain or domains, you can do so by selecting **+Add a domain** and adding the specific DNS suffixes you wish to block. Or if desired, you can add only those domains you wish to permit.

5. Select **Save** to save any changes.

REAL WORLD   **THERE ARE TWO SIDES, AND DNS REQUIREMENTS TOO**

Before your users can have VoIP calls and chat with external users, both SIP domains must have policies that permit the external access. If your organization settings allow all, but the other organization only allows specific domains and yours is not on the list, your users will not be able to communicate with users in the other organization. External access also requires that both domains have the appropriate SRV records in place for Open Federation. See *https://docs.microsoft.com/en-us/microsoft-365/enterprise/external-domain-name-system-records?view=o365-worldwide#external-dns-records-required-for-skype-for-business-online* for more information.

Remove guests

Teams owners can remove guests from their specific teams. When an admin needs to remove a guest user from the organization, they can do so using the Azure Active Directory portal. To do this, follow these steps:

1. Log on to the Azure AD portal at *https://portal.azure.com*.
2. In the Search box, type **users** and then select **Users** under **Services**.
3. You can search or sort or filter for guest users. To filter, select **Add filters** and then select **User type** and select **Apply**.
4. Select **Guest** and select **Apply**.
5. Select the user or users you wish to remove, and select **Delete user**.

Manage Azure AD access review for guests

Access reviews are a powerful tool for reviewing access to Microsoft Teams and other corporate resources. These can be scheduled automatically to force a review of who has access to what, both to ensure that access is still valid and that the people with access still have a need. Access reviews are an Azure AD Premium Plan 2 feature and require either a Global Administrator or a User Administrator to initiate an access review in the Azure AD portal. They can assign any team owner to review the access to their team. To create an access review for all guest users in all teams, do the following:

1. Log on to the Azure AD portal at *https://portal.azure.com*.
2. In the Search box, enter **Identity Governance** and press Enter.
3. In the left menu, select **Access reviews**.
4. Select **+ New access review** to begin.
5. On the first screen, select **Teams + Groups**, and then select the radio button next to **All Microsoft 365 groups with guest users**. Leave the scope set to the default **Guest users only**. Then select **Next: Reviews**. This is shown in Figure 1-28.

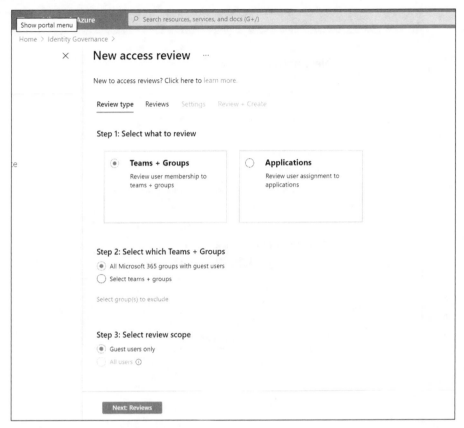

FIGURE 1-28 Settings for guest access review

6. On this screen, you can select who is to perform the review, and how often they should do this. If all Microsoft 365 Groups have owners, you can select **Group owner(s)** to assign the reviews automatically. You can also select a fallback reviewer if any group no longer has an owner.

7. Then select the frequency, the duration (how long the reviewer has to complete the review), and if you wish ,the cycle of review to end at a specific date or after a specific number of iterations. When finished, select **Next: Settings**. Example review options are shown in Figure 1-29.

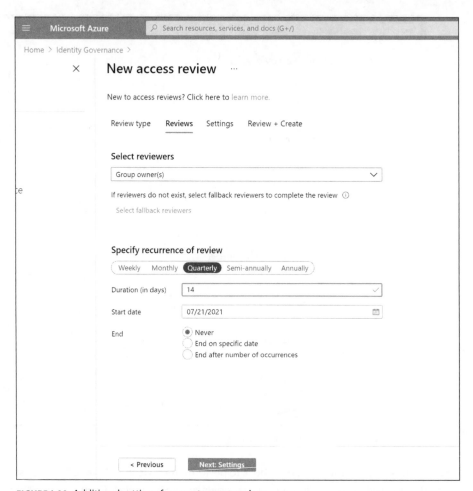

FIGURE 1-29 Additional settings for guest access review

8. On the next screen, you can set actions and responses based on results or lack of response by the group owner, as well as provide additional information to the reviewer, such as the last time a guest actually accessed the content. This can help a reviewer determine if the guest's access is still being used. Examples are shown in Figure 1-30. When you are satisfied with the settings, select **Next: Review + Create**.

FIGURE 1-30 Additional settings for guest access review

9. You can review or make changes on the final screen, and then select **Create** when done. It may take a few moments before the access review you created will show up in the main Access review console.

You can create multiple access reviews if necessary, and adjust them through the Azure portal if assigned reviewers need to change or if you have to revise the frequency or actions. By completing periodic access reviews, you help reduce the chance that someone has access to data they no longer need. This, in turn, helps with the overall security posture of your environment and makes permitting guests access to Teams more palatable to others in your organization who might otherwise be resistant to it.

Configure guest access from Azure AD portal

The last component of guest access in Teams is configuring guest access settings in the Azure AD portal. External collaboration settings are accessible under the Users blade and are specific to overall access, invitations, and allowed/denied domains. To adjust external collaboration settings, do the following:

1. Log on to the Azure portal at *https://portal.azure.com*.

2. Enter **Users** in the search box and press Enter, or select **Users** from the recent shortcuts below the search bar.

3. In the left menu, select **User settings**, and under **External users**, select **Manage external collaboration settings**.

4. Note the options include limiting access to directory data, who can invite guests, and the option to permit or deny specific domains. These are shown in Figure 1-31.

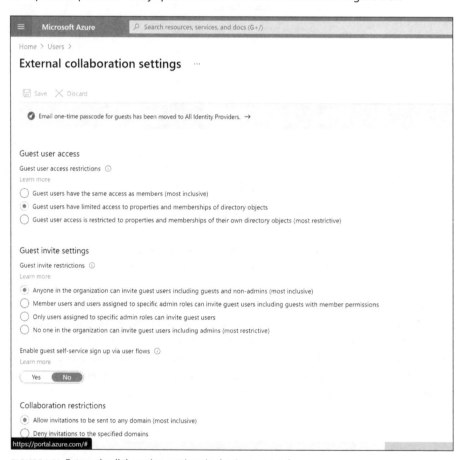

FIGURE 1-31 External collaboration settings in the Azure portal

Skill 1.5: Manage security and compliance

Security and compliance are built into Microsoft 365 and fully integrate across all the Microsoft 365 services. Microsoft Teams, as part of Microsoft 365, takes full advantage of these capabilities and is configured in much the same way as any of the other services, using the same administrative portals. If you are already familiar with security and compliance in Microsoft 365, then you are familiar with it in Microsoft Teams as well. There are just a few things that are specific to Teams you will want to review, but we will look at security and compliance from a Teams perspective in the section "Deploy and manage Microsoft Teams endpoints."

This skill covers how to:

- Assign Microsoft Teams Admin roles
- Create and manage compliance features, including retention policies, sensitivity labels, and data loss prevention (DLP) policies
- Create security and compliance alerts for Microsoft Teams
- Create an information barrier policy

Assign Microsoft Teams Admin roles

Just as with any other Microsoft 365 service, the Global Administrator has full administrative access to Microsoft Teams, and anyone with that role is a Teams administrator. If your organization has service-level admins, there is a Teams Administrator role that you can assign so that an individual can manage Teams, but not have admin rights elsewhere. You should assign the Teams administrator to people who need to do the following:

- Manage all admin features, including voice and telephony in the Teams & Skype admin center and Teams PowerShell modules

- Add and manage Microsoft 365 groups
- Open and manage service requests
- Monitor service health

To make a user a Teams administrator, follow these steps:

1. Log on to the Microsoft 365 admin portal at *https://admin.microsoft.com*.
2. In the left menu, select **Show all** and then select **Roles**.
3. In the Azure **AD pane**, select **Teams Administrator**.
4. In the **Teams Administrator** fly-out, select the **Assigned admins** tab.
5. Select **+Add** and select the users you want to make Teams admins. Select **Save** when done.

There are other Teams admin roles that support different levels of administrative control and the principle of least privilege. Table 1-6 lists all the admin roles and their associated abilities.

TABLE 1-6 Teams Admin roles

Role	Tasks
Teams Administrator	Administer all aspects of Microsoft Teams
Teams Communications Administrator	Administer calling and meetings features, including policies, configurations, conference bridges, and the Call Quality Dashboard (CQD)
Teams Communications Support Engineer	Troubleshoot communications issues across the service, including org-wide details in the CQD
Teams Communications Support Specialist	Troubleshoot individual communications issues for users, including user-specific details in the CQD
Teams Device Administrator	Manage all certified devices being used with Teams using the TAC or PowerShell

> **REAL WORLD**   **TEAMS ADMINISTRATOR VERSUS GLOBAL ADMINISTRATOR**
>
> While users who are in the Teams Administrator role can manage all Teams (and Skype for Business Online) features and settings, they may not be able to do everything related to Teams. In the section about Guest Access, we saw settings that needed to be made in Azure, Microsoft 365, and SharePoint. If you are a Teams administrator but not a Global Administrator, you may need other admins to help you make those settings.

Create and manage compliance features, including retention policies, sensitivity labels, and data loss prevention (DLP) policies

As mentioned earlier, Microsoft Teams is a part of Microsoft 365, so features that cover security and compliance are integrated with the rest of the services in Microsoft 365. Retention policies, sensitivity labels, and DLP policies can all be set for the Microsoft 365 services as a unified policy, though you can set different policies if you need to. Some customers prefer a longer retention for email, and a (much) shorter retention for chats, but not for channel messages. To create a retention policy specific to Microsoft Teams, do the following:

1. Log on to the Microsoft 365 Compliance portal at *https://compliance.microsoft.com*.

2. In the left menu, select **Policies**.

3. Under **Data**, select **Retention**.

4. Select **+New retention policy** to create a policy.

5. Name the policy and provide a description. Then select **Next**.

6. In the locations panel, turn off all the defaults, and turn on **Teams chats**, as shown in Figure 1-32.

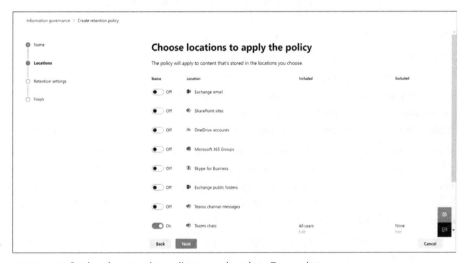

FIGURE 1-32 Setting the retention policy to apply only to Teams chats

7. You can adjust settings for specific users or exempt specific users. Make any necessary changes, and then select **Next**.

8. Set the period for retention, and specify what to do when the period is over. To remove chats over one year old, you need to choose the **Delete items automatically** option, as shown in Figure 1-33.

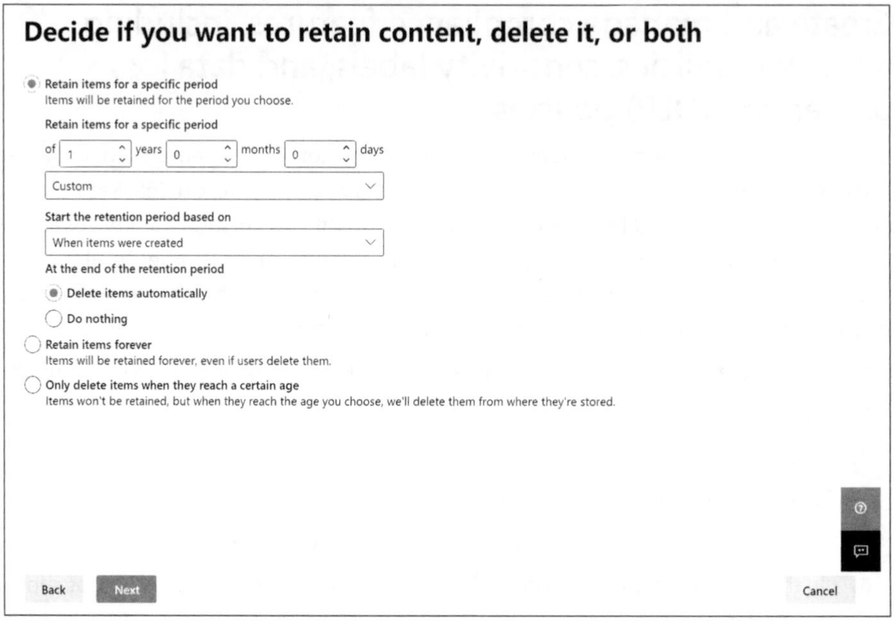

Decide if you want to retain content, delete it, or both

⦿ Retain items for a specific period
Items will be retained for the period you choose.

Retain items for a specific period

of [1] years [0] months [0] days

[Custom   ∨]

Start the retention period based on

[When items were created   ∨]

At the end of the retention period
⦿ Delete items automatically
◯ Do nothing

◯ Retain items forever
Items will be retained forever, even if users delete them.

◯ Only delete items when they reach a certain age
Items won't be retained, but when they reach the age you choose, we'll delete them from where they're stored.

[Back] [Next]   Cancel

FIGURE 1-33 Setting the retention policy for one year, with automatic deletion

9. Select **Next**.

10. Review the settings, make any necessary changes, and then select **Submit**.

Note that the shortest retention period for Teams message content is 1 day. But due to the way the managed folder assistant works, the shortest practical retention period is one week, and a mailbox must be great than 10MB. See *https://docs.microsoft.com/en-US/office365/ troubleshoot/archive-mailboxes/message-not-moved-to-archive* for more information.

Sensitivity labels are used across Microsoft Teams, Microsoft 365 Groups, and in SharePoint to classify and protect data. Specific to Teams, customers may use sensitivity labels to ensure that in scenarios where they are permitting guest access, guests cannot access content that is labeled appropriately even if another user adds content to a team that has guests. To create and use an "Internal Only" sensitivity label with Teams, do the following:

1. In the Compliance center, select **Show All**, and then under **Solutions**, select **Information Protection**.

2. Select **+Create a label** to create a new label. Fill out the required fields and then select **Next**.

3. Ensure that **Files & emails** and **Groups & sites** are both selected, and then select **Next**.

4. If desired, set encryption or marking of files and emails, and then select **Next**.

5. If desired, set up auto-labeling conditions so that the label can be automatically applied to data that matches the condition(s) you set. Then select **Next**.

6. Select the options **Privacy and external user access settings** and **External sharing and Conditional Access settings** and then select **Next**.

7. In the **Define privacy and external user access settings**, set **Privacy** to **Private**, as shown in Figure 1-34, then select **Next**.

FIGURE 1-34 Setting the privacy to Private

8. In the **Define external sharing and device access settings**, choose **Only people in your organization** as shown in Figure 1-35, then select **Next**.

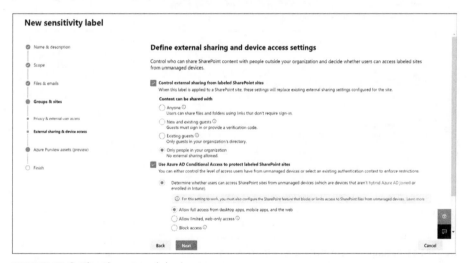

FIGURE 1-35 Setting the external sharing to none

9. Select **Next**.

10. Select **Create label**.

11. Before you can use this, you will need to follow the steps in the final screen. Select **Publish this label**.

12. Select **Choose sensitivity labels to publish**, select the label you created earlier, and select **Add**. Then select **Next**.

13. By default, this label will be published to all users and groups. Make changes if necessary, then select **Next**.

14. If desired, you can apply this label by default and make settings to control this. For this purpose, just select **Next**.

15. Name your policy and add an optional description, then select **Next**.

16. Review and, if necessary, edit your settings; then select **Submit**, and then **Done**.

17. If you wish to automatically apply the label to anything, select the **Automatically apply** link. Otherwise, the label will be available for applying manually to content and sites when desired.

To apply the **Internal Only** label to a new team, choose the sensitivity label from the drop-down list as shown in Figure 1-36.

FIGURE 1-36 Setting the sensitivity label for a new team

REAL WORLD   LICENSING IMPLICATIONS

There are licensing implications when using sensitivity labels. Make sure you review *https:// docs.microsoft.com/en-us/office365/servicedescriptions/microsoft-365-service-descriptions/ microsoft-365-tenantlevel-services-licensing-guidance/microsoft-365-security-compliance- licensing-guidance* and secure the correct licensing for the features you wish to use.

To modify an existing team to use the sensitivity label, do the following:

1. Select the ellipsis button for the team and select **Edit team**.

2. From the Sensitivity drop-down, select the Sensitivity label you created earlier, as shown in Figure 1-37.

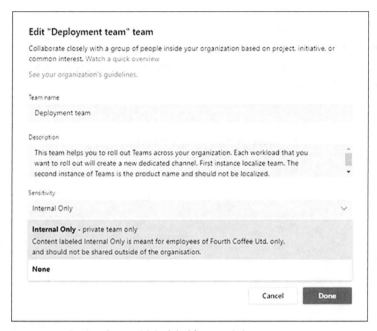

FIGURE 1-37 Setting the sensitivity label for an existing team

3. Select **Done**.

EXAM TIP

Before you can apply sensitivity labels to Microsoft Teams, you need to synchronize your labels to Azure AD. To do so, connect to the Security & Compliance Center PowerShell (Connect-IPPSSession) and run the cmdlet Execute-AzureAdLabelSync. It may take several minutes for this change to take effect. You will also need to enable support for sensitivity labels. See *https://docs.microsoft.com/en-us/azure/active-directory/enterprise-users/groups-assign-sensitivity-labels* for details.

You can use DLP policies in Teams to help prevent accidental data loss or spillage. DLP policies applied to SharePoint sites and OneDrive accounts protect the files in Teams. Customers with an E5 license, the Information Protection and Governance License, or the Advanced Compliance License can also apply DLP policies to chats and channels. You can edit an existing DLP policy to include Teams chat and channel messages, or you can create a new policy. To update an existing DLP policy for email, SharePoint sites and OneDrive accounts to include Teams chat and channel messages, follow these steps:

1. Log on to the **Compliance Portal** at *https://compliance.microsoft.com*.

2. In the left menu, select **Show all** and then under **Solutions** select **Data loss prevention**.

3. Select the policy you want to now apply to Teams chats and channel messages, and then select **Edit policy**.

4. Select **Next** to get to the **Locations to apply the policy** tab. Set **Teams chat and channel messages** to **On**, as shown in Figure 1-38.

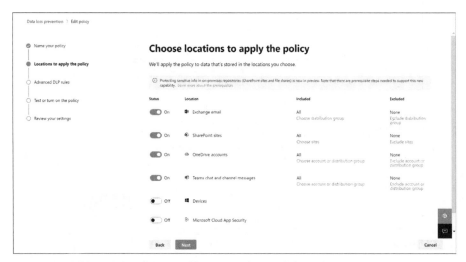

FIGURE 1-38 Editing a DLP policy to apply to Teams chats and channel messages

5. Select **Next** three times to get to the end, and then select **Submit**.

REAL WORLD   **MICROSOFT TEAMS AND DLP LICENSING**

Microsoft Teams stores files in either SharePoint or OneDrive for Business, and DLP is available in those services with the E3 (or equivalent) licensing. DLP can also be used with real-time chat, but to get that, you need the E5 (or equivalent) licensing, or one of the following add-ons: Microsoft 365 Information Protection and Governance or Office 365 Advanced Compliance. Also be aware that although DLP can block messages that contain content that matches a DLP policy, that will not affect activity notifications, which can include a short message preview. So if the content that matches is in the first few words of a chat, it may be visible to users even if the full message itself is blocked. There are also requirements for Teams Only mode. Both the sender and the receiver must be in Teams Only mode, and in cross-org communications you must be using native Teams federation.

Create security and compliance alerts for Microsoft Teams

Security and compliance alerts in Microsoft 365 can be used to help admins monitor what is happening in Teams. Auditing is available in the Microsoft 365 Compliance Center and can alert you about several activities within Teams, including those related to changes to team, channel, connector, member, organization, and other activities. See *https://docs.microsoft.com/en-us/microsoftteams/audit-log-events#teams-activities* for a complete list. Auditing is on by default in Microsoft 365. Several of these auditing events correspond to activities in SharePoint or OneDrive for Business as well. To use auditing to view activities in Microsoft Teams, do the following:

1. Log on to the **Microsoft Compliance Center** at *https://compliance.microsoft.com*.

2. On the left, select **Audit**.

3. Select **Activities**, and in the Search box under Activities, type **teams**. You will see a list of Microsoft Teams activities and Microsoft Teams Shifts activities that are audited, as shown in Figure 1-39.

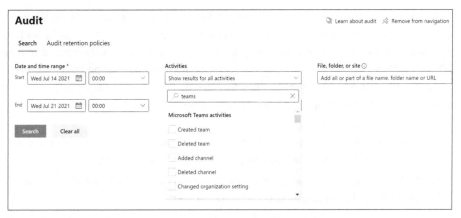

FIGURE 1-39 Activities that can be audited specific to Microsoft Teams

4. Select one or more activities that you wish to review, set the date range, specify users (optional,) and select **Search**.

5. Review the audit log. You can select **Export** to save the results as a CSV file if desired.

Create an information barrier policy

Information barriers can be used by customers who need to prevent communications between certain groups of their users. An information barrier policy can be useful when regulatory or compliance requirements involving financial transactions are in play, or when an organization has two customers who are competitors and must ensure there is no sharing of information between its own users that could compromise their customers' proprietary information. Sometimes referred to as *ethical walls*, information barriers in Teams can prevent the following activities:

- Searching for a user
- Adding a member to a team

- Starting a chat session with someone
- Starting a group chat
- Inviting someone to join a meeting
- Sharing a screen
- Placing a call
- Sharing a file with another user
- Accessing a file through a sharing link

Information barriers in Microsoft Teams are bidirectional. You cannot have one user or group be able to communicate with another but block the reverse. Each user protected by information barriers also requires E5 or equivalent licensing, or the Advanced Compliance or Insider Risk Management add-on licenses. Information barriers can also be used to allow communications in the event you have a situation where it is more straightforward to define who users *can* communicate with, rather than who they cannot.

To use information barriers, you must first define an attribute in Azure Active Directory that will identify populations. If you are synchronizing data from your on-premises Active Directory, this means ensuring that data is properly populated in AD and synchronizing to Azure AD. Although you can define multiple segments for use with information barriers, a single user can only belong to a single segment. Keep this in mind if a manager has employees who must have information barriers applied to them. Setting up information barriers is accomplished as follows:

1. Populate users' accounts with an attribute in Azure AD (synced from on-prem) to segment users. Remember, a user can belong to only one segment.

2. Define the segments needed in your organization, using the PowerShell cmdlet **New-OrganizationSegment**.

3. Define the policies and whether they are block or allow policies, using the PowerShell cmdlet **New-InformationBarrierPolicy**.

4. Activate the information barrier policies, using the PowerShell cmdlet **Set-InformationBarrierPolicy**.

5. Apply the information barrier policies, using the PowerShell cmdlet **Start-InformationBarrierPoliciesApplication**.

Although the attribute values used are defined in your on-prem Active Directory and then synchronized to Azure AD, or defined directly in Azure AD if there is no on-premises AD, all of the management of information barriers is done through PowerShell. Also, note that it can take a few minutes to several hours for information barrier policies to become effective, depending on the size of your organization and the number of users involved.

See *https://docs.microsoft.com/en-us/microsoft-365/compliance/information-barriers-policies?view=o365-worldwide* for more details.

Skill 1.6: Deploy and manage Microsoft Teams endpoints

In this skill section, we will look at what it takes to deploy client software and manage endpoints, including both client devices and Microsoft Teams Rooms hardware.

> **This skill covers how to:**
> - Deploy Microsoft Teams clients to devices, including Windows, VDI (Virtual Desktop), Windows Virtual Desktop (WVD), MacOS, and mobile devices
> - Manage configuration profiles
> - Manage Microsoft Teams device tags
> - Manage device settings and firmware
> - Configure Microsoft Teams Rooms

Deploy Microsoft Teams clients to devices, including Windows, VDI (Virtual Desktop), Windows Virtual Desktop (WVD), MacOS, and mobile devices

Microsoft Teams can be accessed with nothing more than a supported web browser, but there are fully featured rich clients for Windows, Mac, Linux, iOS/iPadOS, and Android. For Windows, Mac, and Linux, users with platform-appropriate local administrator rights can install the client on their device themselves, or administrators can deploy clients using enterprise management tools such as Microsoft Intune or Microsoft Endpoint Configuration Manager, JAMF, or Linux software distribution solutions like Yum. Mobile users must be able to install apps on their devices themselves from their platform's app store. On Windows, users do not require admin rights, but they do on Macs and require root privileges to deploy on Linux, and they must be able to deploy software to their mobile devices directly.

The desktop client for Windows is available as a stand-alone product and is also included in the installer for Microsoft 365 Apps for Enterprise. It comes in both 32- and 64-bit versions, and it is supported on all currently supported Windows platforms, currently supported Mac platforms, and on Linux distros that can use RPM or DEB packages.

It is also important to note that there are no central configuration options for managing the Teams client through features like Group Policy or with configuration files. You can manage Microsoft Teams features and capabilities through the TAC or PowerShell, but client-side settings will need to be specified by the individual users.

The mobile clients can be installed from the respective mobile platform's app stores only. Separate packages for installation through mobile device management (MDM) or by side-loading are not available and are not supported by Microsoft.

Once installed, the Teams client updates itself. Updates are checked for automatically and applied by the client automatically on all platforms. Managing or delaying updates to the Teams client is not supported because access to an evolving cloud service like Teams requires the client to be updated regularly to enable new features and to provide security and bug fixes.

On VDI (Virtual Desktop), you can use Microsoft Teams for chat and collaboration. Calling and meeting functionality requires that you use the Windows Virtual Desktop, Citrix, or VMware platforms. Media optimizations are required for calling and meetings, and there is a significant difference between using persistent and nonpersistent VDI. In persistent VDI, you can use either a per-user or a per-machine installation. In per-user, Teams updates itself just as it does on other platforms. But in the per-machine installation, which is required for nonpersistent VDI, updates are disabled. To update the Teams client in a nonpersistent environment (which requires the use of per-machine installation), you must uninstall Teams and then install from the latest version. Microsoft Teams updates very frequently, so be sure to consider this when determining whether to use nonpersistent VDI and/or whether to have users of nonpersistent VDI use the rich client or the web client.

> **NEED MORE REVIEW?   CLIENT DEPLOYMENT DETAILS**
>
> For more detailed instructions on client deployment, see *https://docs.microsoft.com/en-us/microsoftteams/get-clients.*

Manage configuration profiles

Configuration profiles refer specifically to Microsoft Teams hardware devices and provide you with a way to manage them from the TAC. Configuration profiles can be used to manage the following types of devices:

- Collaboration bars
- Conference phones
- Desk phones
- Microsoft Teams Rooms
- Teams displays
- Teams panels

What specific things you can set with a configuration profile will depend on the device type and the features the vendor has implemented, but may include the following:

- Device information
- Managing updates and upgrades
- Policies

- Tags
- Reboots
- Diagnostics

To manage configuration profiles, you must first create them, and then assign them to specific devices. To do so, follow these steps:

1. Log on to the TAC at *https://admin.teams.microsoft.com*.

2. In the left menu, expand **Devices**.

3. Select the device type you want to configure, and then select **Configuration profiles**.

4. Select **+Add** to create a new configuration profile.

5. Review and update the settings as appropriate for your device. You can have multiple device configuration profiles, so for example if you have offices in different time zones, you can set profiles up per time zone so that the clock will display the correct local time. See Figure 1-40 for an example.

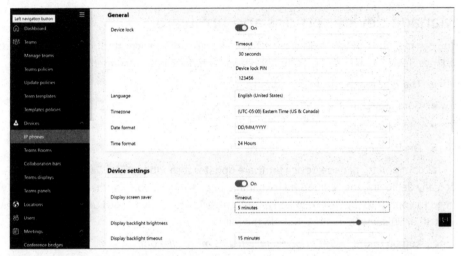

FIGURE 1-40 A configuration profile for an IP phone

6. Select **Save**.

7. On the device screen, select **Assigned devices** to apply the configuration profile to the device(s) you choose.

Manage Microsoft Teams device tags

Tags apply to all devices and are linked to user accounts that are used to sign in to a device. They are used to organize devices in your organization and to help with identifying a location, grouping and filtering devices, applying software updates, and monitoring call quality. You can create tags for whatever grouping you find useful for monitoring or filtering devices in your organization. You can create, modify, or delete tags; add, remove, or modify them on a single or multiple devices; and then use tags as a search, sort, or filter category when looking at multiple devices. To manage Microsoft Teams device tags, follow these steps:

1. Log on to the TAC at *https://admin.teams.microsoft.com*.

2. In the left menu, select **Devices** and then select the device type for which you want to manage tags. Tags, once created, are available to all devices.

3. Select **Actions** and then **All device tags**.

4. Select **+Add** to create a new tag. You can create a tag with up to 25 alphanumeric characters. You can also select an existing tag to edit or delete if necessary. When done, select **Save**.

5. Select the device or devices you wish to manage, and then select **Manage tags**.

6. Assign the tag you wish to the device(s) and then select **Apply**.

Now you can select the Filter icon to filter the list of devices to those with the tag you select.

Manage device settings and firmware

You can manage updates to Microsoft Teams–compatible devices through the TAC, including phones, Teams panels, and collaboration bars. Updates can be managed for the following:

- The Teams app and Teams admin agent
- Company portal app
- OEM agent app
- Device firmware

It's common to manage device firmware updates through the TAC. When you do, you are actually deploying the N-1 update to manageable devices. If you want the N version, you will need to apply it to the device directly. You can decide to apply the N-1 update immediately, or wait 30 or 90 days. To manage this, do the following:

1. Log on to the TAC at *https://admin.teams.microsoft.com*.

2. In the left menu, select **Devices**, and then select the type of device.

3. Select the device or devices you wish to update.

4. Select **Update**.

5. Choose the update option you wish to deploy.

6. Select **Update**.

To revert an update, you will need to perform a factory reset on the device per the manufacturer's instructions.

Configure Microsoft Teams Rooms

Microsoft Teams Rooms (MTR) are meeting and conference rooms equipped with specific hardware to accommodate meetings in Teams (as well as other supported platforms). They typically include a control panel/device, a large display, one or more cameras, speaker and microphone setups, and the capability to directly connect laptops to share content. Hardware is available from hardware manufacturers such as Yealink, Logitech, Poly, Lenovo, and HP. The hardware typically runs the MTR console application on top of Windows 10. The MTR connects to Microsoft Teams with a user account that is associated with the specific room, which facilitates scheduling meetings in the room using Outlook or Microsoft Teams. Compatible hardware also offers Bluetooth beaconing so that users can one-touch join meetings using their mobile device when entering a room.

Configuring an MTR involves setting up the following:

1. User account (UPN) and password for the account used by the device.
2. The SIP domain if different from the user account UPN domain.
3. The default hardware to use, including
   a. Microphone for conferencing
   b. Speaker for conferencing
   c. Default speaker for device audio, used for devices connected to the HDMI ingest.
   d. (Optional) Presentation camera, if connected.

Once configured, the MTR should automatically launch and connect.

Configuring the MTR using TAC provides additional options, including the wallpaper theme, whether or not to use Cortana, whether or not the MTR can be used to join Cisco Webex and Zoom meetings, and whether or not to use Modern Authentication. To configure an MTR, follow these steps.

1. Log on to the TAC at *https://admin.teams.microsoft.com*.
2. On the left navigation, expand **Devices** and then select **Teams Rooms**.
3. Select the MTR you wish to configure, and then select **Edit settings**.
4. Enter the settings you wish for the MTR device, as shown in Figure 1-41.

FIGURE 1-41 Editing settings for an MTR

Changes will apply after the device restarts. You can remotely force or reschedule a restart if required.

Skill 1.7: Monitor and analyze service usage

The final skill in this chapter has to do with monitoring and analyzing service usage, which can include both monitoring active usage by your users, measuring quality, and troubleshooting issues. Microsoft Teams has a variety of tools and reports to assist you with these tasks, and we will review them here.

This skill covers how to:

- Interpret Microsoft Teams usage reports
- Interpret Microsoft 365 usage reports
- Optimize call quality by using Call Analytics
- Analyze organization-wide call quality by using Call Quality Dashboard
- Use Power BI to identify call quality issues

Interpret Microsoft Teams usage reports

The TAC includes several analytic and reporting options for Microsoft Teams. Global Admins and Teams Service admins can view these reports, which go into greater detail than the usage reports in the Microsoft 365 admin center. Reports include detailed usage, activities, devices, meetings, and callings reports. Microsoft Teams offers several usage reports, including the following:

- Teams usage report
- Teams user activity report
- Teams device usage report
- Teams Live Event usage report
- Teams PSTN blocked users report
- Teams PSTN minute pools report
- Teams PSTN usage report-Calling Plans
- Teams PSTN usage report-Direct Routing

To view usage reports, do the following:

1. Log on to the TAC at *https://admin.teams.microsoft.com*.
2. In the left menu, expand **Analytics & reports**, and select **Usage reports**.
3. From the **Select report** drop-down list, choose the report you wish to view.
4. From the **Date range** drop-down list, select the date range.
5. Select **Run report**. The selected report will display, as shown in Figure 1-42.

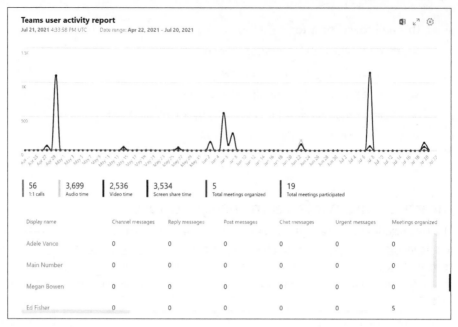

FIGURE 1-42 The Teams user activity report

In the report, you can see users' activity across chat, 1:1 calls, meetings, and so forth, and drill in on any single user you wish to examine.

> **NEED MORE REVIEW? DATA PRIVACY**
>
> User privacy concerns can be addressed by anonymizing data in this report. See *https://docs.microsoft.com/en-us/microsoftteams/teams-analytics-and-reports/teams-reporting-reference#make-the-user-specific-data-anonymous*.

Interpret Microsoft 365 usage reports

The Microsoft 365 usage reports are complementary to the Microsoft Teams usage reports and are intended to provide admins with an overview of the total usage of Microsoft 365, rather than detailed insight into each service. You can see some of the same information, but the emphasis is on overall adoption. To view the Microsoft 365 usage report specific to Microsoft Teams, do the following:

1. Log on to the Microsoft 365 admin center at *https://admin.microsoft.com*.
2. In the left menu, select **Show all**, expand **Reports**, and then select **Usage**.
3. Scroll down until you see the **Microsoft Teams activity** report.
4. Select the **View more** button.
5. By default, you will see a 30-day history on the **User activity** tab, as shown in Figure 1-43.

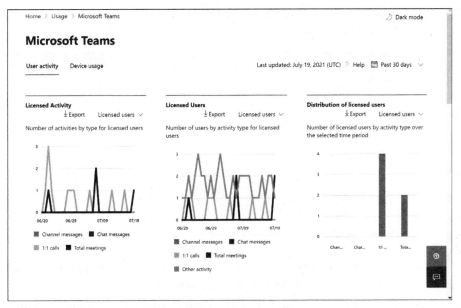

FIGURE 1-43 The Microsoft Teams usage report

6. You can select 7, 30, 90, or 180 days. You can select the **Device usage** tab to see a break-down of device usage.

7. You can export any of the summary reports as a CSV file if desired.

Optimize call quality by using Call Analytics

Teams administrators can use Call Analytics to monitor, analyze, and troubleshoot Teams call quality and connection problems for individual users. This is useful for dealing with individual calls of specific users, rather than looking at the overall service health. Call Analytics access can be enhanced with physical site information, and access can be granted to Call Analytics for help desk or other support personnel without having to grant them a broader Teams adminis-trative role. To use Call Analytics, you must first set it up, which involves two steps:

1. Grant access to the appropriate support personnel. There are two in-built administra-tive roles in Microsoft Teams focused on this. The **Teams communication support specialist** role is typically for tier 1 support personnel and gives them a limited view of Call Analytics. The **Teams communications support engineer** role is intended for tier 2 support personnel and gives those users full access to Call Analytics. Neither role has any access to any other part of Microsoft Teams administration. You can assign users to these roles using the Azure Active Directory portal by doing the following:

    a. Log on to the Azure Active Directory portal at h*ttps://portal.azure.com*.

    b. In the search box, enter **roles** and select **Azure AD roles and administrators** from the list.

   c. In the search box, enter **Teams**. You will then see a filtered list of the Microsoft Teams admin roles, as shown in Figure 1-44.

FIGURE 1-44 Microsoft administrative roles

   d. Select the role you wish to add a user to, and select **+Add assignments**. Select the user or users you wish to add, and then select **Select**.

   e. Select **Next**, then select **Active**, enter **justification**, and then select **Assign**.

2. Upload information about your environment to Microsoft Teams. A CSV file can map IP subnets in your organization to specific offices, floors, and so forth to help correlate users with physical locations and network connectivity. See *https://docs.microsoft.com/en-us/microsoftteams/cqd-upload-tenant-building-data* for details on how to create the CSV and upload it to Microsoft Teams.

Once you complete these steps, you are ready to use Call Analytics. Call Analytics shows detailed information about specific users' individual calls. As such, you access it through the individual user.

1. Log on to the TAC at *https://admin.teams.microsoft.com*.

2. In the left menu, select **Users**.

3. Select the user whose Call Analytics you wish to review.

4. In the user information, select the **Meetings & calls** tab. You will see each of the user's calls.

5. Select a specific call.

6. View specifics about the call, including start and end date/time, call quality, network details, system details, and hardware used, as shown in Figure 1-45.

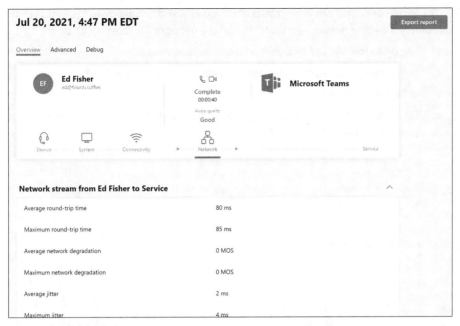

FIGURE 1-45 Call Analytics

7. The Overview tab provides an overview, whereas the Advanced tab provides more details in a list format. The Debug tab can provide information useful to Microsoft support if you engage them for assistance. You can export any of the information by selecting **Export report**.

8. With details of the call, you can determine if call quality issues were caused by network conditions, hardware issues, and so forth by reviewing each aspect of the call.

Analyze organization-wide call quality by using Call Quality Dashboard

The Call Quality Dashboard (CQD) provides a more holistic view of the overall performance of Microsoft Teams for your organization. As with Call Analytics, CQD is more useful if you have uploaded network information for your organization. Using CQD, Microsoft Teams admins can view reports about the following:

- Overall call quality
- Server-client connectivity
- Client-client connectivity
- Voice quality SLA

For each report, you can view graphs of call quality, with breakdowns for wired versus wireless, and "Inside" the network versus "Outside" the network. To access CQD, do the following:

1. Log on to the TAC at *https://admin.teams.microsoft.com*.

2. In the left menu, select **Call quality dashboard** to open a new tab.

3. In the upper-right corner, select **Sign In**.

4. On the **Overall Call Quality** tab, review the call quality metrics for each of the call types, as shown in Figure 1-46.

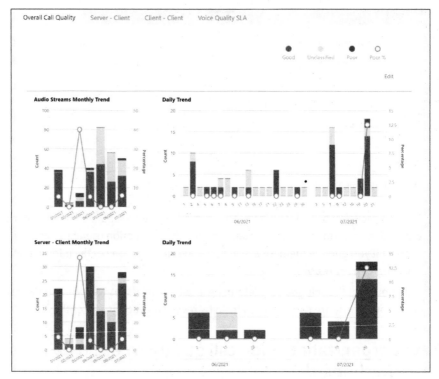

FIGURE 1-46 Viewing CQD for overall call quality

> **NEED MORE REVIEW?** **USING CQD HOW-TO**
>
> See *https://docs.microsoft.com/en-us/MicrosoftTeams/quality-of-experience-review-guide* for more on how to use CQD.

Use Power BI to identify call quality issues

For detailed analysis of data, nothing beats Power BI. The Microsoft Teams Utilization reports provide insight into Teams usage and overall call quality, and they include the following reports:

- Call Count Summary
- Audio Minutes Summary
- Usage
- Conference Details
- Regional Audio Details
- User List

To use Power BI, you need a Power BI license and to install the Power BI application on your Windows desktop. Then, do the following:

1. Download the Power BI Connector for Microsoft Advanced Call Quality Dashboard from *https://github.com/MicrosoftDocs/OfficeDocs-SkypeForBusiness/blob/live/Teams/ downloads/CQD-Power-BI-query-templates.zip?raw=true*.

2. Place the MicrosoftCallQuality.pqx file in the %Documents%\Power BI Desktop\Custom Connectors folder. If this folder does not exist, create it.

3. Launch Power BI. On the Home tab, select **Get Data**.

4. Browse to **Online Services** and select **Microsoft Call Quality.**

5. When prompted, sign in to your tenant with your administrative account.

6. Select **Load** to complete the process.

You will see available data from which to create queries for further analysis or to create dashboards. The download also includes several PBIT files for pulling more information out of CQD, including these:

- Helpdesk Report
- Location Enhanced Report
- Mobile Device Report
- PSTN Report
- Summary Report
- Teams Usage Report
- User Feedback Report

Each of these can provide very detailed information about a user, location, and so forth. Figure 1-47 shows the User Activities tab from the Helpdesk Report template.

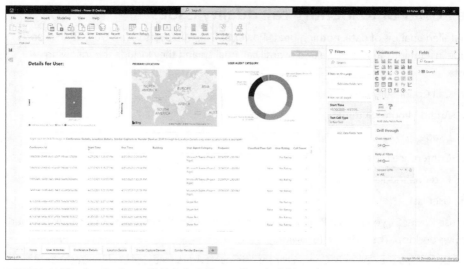

FIGURE 1-47 Viewing the Power BI Helpdesk Report, User Activities tab

Chapter summary

- Upgrading from Skype for Business to Microsoft Teams offers several options and compatibility modes to meet an organization's needs.
- Properly configuring the networks your clients use is critical to ensuring excellent performance with Microsoft Teams.
- Governance and lifecycle management involves management of groups as well as data retention.
- Guest access can be controlled in very granular fashion to support collaboration and security.
- Security and compliance are built into Microsoft Teams.
- Deploying client software varies from computer to mobile device and from end user to room hardware.
- Reporting and tools, including the Call Quality Dashboard and Power BI, should be used to monitor Microsoft Teams usage and ensure best performance.

Thought experiment

In this thought experiment, demonstrate your skills and knowledge of the topics covered in this chapter. You can find the answers in the section that follows.

Skill 1.1: Upgrade from Skype for Business to Microsoft Teams

1. You need to install the Microsoft Teams client to your Windows computers currently running the Skype for Business client with minimal effort. What is the best way to do this?

    a. Use a Group Policy Object to install the software.

    b. Publish the Microsoft Teams application using Intune and prompt users to install.

    c. Use the Skype for Business Admin Console to update the UX to Teams Mode.

    d. Use the Teams Admin Center to set "Download the Teams app in the background for Skype for Business users" to On.

2. You are preparing to migrate your organization from Skype for Business to Microsoft Teams. You want your users to use Skype for Business for meetings and chat, but to start using Microsoft Teams for additional functionality. How should you do this?

    a. Create a Teams Client Policy package and apply it to users.

    b. Use PowerShell to set Teams and Skype for Business to run in Islands Mode.

    c. Set the coexistence mode to SfBWithTeamsCollab.

    d. Stop the Collaboration Service on the Skype for Business servers.

3. You have federation with a partner organization for instant messaging with Skype for Business. You are planning to migrate to Microsoft Teams and want to make sure that you can continue to communicate with the partner organization that will keep using Skype for Business. What do you need to do in order to ensure that instant messaging capabilities are not interrupted?

    a. Confirm that the partner organization and you are both using Open Federation.

    b. Export the certificate from your Skype for Business server(s) and import it to Microsoft Teams.

    c. Nothing; instant messaging federation is transitive.

    d. Update the external collaboration settings in Azure Active Directory to permit the partner org's federation.

Skill 1.2: Plan and configure network settings for Microsoft Teams

1. You configure your firewall to permit outbound traffic to Microsoft Teams networks over TCP 443. Users report poor-quality audio during Teams calls. You take a network trace and see traffic over TCP port 443 is working fine. What should you do next?

    a. Update the firewall to allow outbound traffic to UDP 3478-3481.

    b. Configure the Teams clients to use a proxy server for faster access.

    c. Install the SILK codec to operating system.

    d. Rerun the Network Planner in the Teams Admin Center to optimize your routes.

2. Users on a busy network segment are complaining about poor-quality audio and video during Teams meetings. Which of the following options would be the best change to try first to improve the situation?

   a. Have the users join Teams meetings using the Web Client.

   b. Use the Microsoft Teams Admin Center to enable QoS.

   c. Edit the firewall rules so that TCP traffic is evaluated before UDP traffic.

   d. Create a new VLAN and move the users to this VLAN.

3. During your pilot of Microsoft Teams, you need to identify if there is any packet loss from pilot users' computers. Which tool would you use to do this most efficiently?

   a. Microsoft Teams Network Testing Companion

   b. Microsoft Teams Call Quality Dashboard

   c. Microsoft Teams Call Analytics

   d. Power BI with the Microsoft Teams Connector

Skill 1.3: Implement governance and lifecycle management for Microsoft Teams

1. You need to configure Teams so that each team must expire in one year and all team content is deleted when the team expires. Where would you do this?

   a. In the Teams Admin Center, Teams, properties of the Team.

   b. In the Security & Compliance Center, Retention Policies.

   c. In the Azure Portal, Groups, Expiration.

   d. In the Teams Admin Center, Policy Packages, create and apply a policy that includes expiration.

2. You need to configure a specific team so that it is identified as Highly Confidential in the Teams client. How would you do this?

   a. Use the Teams client to display a banner for the team.

   b. Create a Sensitivity Label in the Security & Compliance Center and then edit the settings for the team.

   c. Configure the team to be Private.

   d. Apply the Team template "Highly Confidential" to the team.

3. You need to ensure that guest memberships in Microsoft Teams are reviewed on a regular basis by the Team owners. What can you use to do this?

   a. Azure Active Directory Access Reviews

   b. Compliance Reviews

   c. Microsoft Teams membership reviews

   d. Office 365 Group Reviews

Skill 1.4: Configure and manage guest access

1. You wish to configure Microsoft Teams to allow Guest Access. Your company has a security policy that specifies guests can only come from specific domains. Where would you configure this?

   a. The Teams Admin Center, Org-wide Settings, Guest access.

   b. The Microsoft 365 Admin Center, Settings, Domains.

   c. The Azure Portal, Users, User settings, External users.

   d. The Security & Compliance Center, External Access, Domains.

2. You wish to configure Microsoft Teams so that guest users cannot turn on their camera during meetings. Where would you configure this?

   a. The Teams Admin Center, Users, Guest policies.

   b. The Teams Admin Center, Meetings, Meeting policies.

   c. The Teams Admin Center, Org-wide Settings, External access.

   d. The Teams Admin Center, Org-wide Settings, Guest access.

3. You need to review what guest users can access in your Teams environment. How could you do this?

   a. In the Azure Portal, Identity Governance, Access reviews.

   b. In the Teams Admin Center, Users, Guest user access report.

   c. In the Security & Compliance Center, Investigations, Access reviews.

   d. In the Azure Portal, Audit, Guest access audit report.

Skill 1.5: Manage security and compliance

1. You need to ensure that a user cannot permanently delete 1:1 chat messages. How would you do this?

   a. Create a retention policy for Teams chats.

   b. Place the user's mailbox on an in-place hold.

   c. Create a Teams Meeting policy and apply it to the user.

   d. Create a Teams Client policy and apply it to the user.

2. You need to configure Teams so that a user can manage meetings settings for Teams. What role should you assign them?

   a. Teams Communications Administrator

   b. Teams Communications Support Engineer

   c. Teams Communications Support Specialist

   d. Teams Service Administrator

3. You need to configure Teams meetings so that guest users cannot use their webcam. How would you do this?

   a. In the Microsoft Teams Admin Center, under Meetings, use a Meetings policy.

   b. In the Microsoft Teams Admin Center, under Org-wide Settings, modify the Guest Access Settings.

   c. In the Microsoft Teams Admin Center, under Org-wide Settings, modify the Teams settings.

   d. In the Azure AD portal, under Users, Guest User restrictions, modify the video policy.

Skill 1.6: Deploy and manage Microsoft Teams endpoints

1. You have a group of users using Microsoft Teams on nonpersistent VDIs. They notice that users of physical workstations have new features in Teams that they do not. What do you need to do to fix this?

   a. Uninstall Microsoft Teams client from the VDI master image and then reinstall it.

   b. Use the PowerShell cmdlet Grant-CsTeamsUpgradePolicy to update the users.

   c. Configure Automatic Updates.

   d. Instruct the users to use the Check For Updates option in the Microsoft Teams client.

2. Your users all use Microsoft Windows desktops that are fully updated and Azure AD joined. They are enrolled in Intune as well. Users do not have local administrative access. You need to deploy the Microsoft Teams client to all desktops. How should you do this?

   a. Send a link to download and install the client to all users, since Microsoft Teams does not require local admin rights to install.

   b. Create a Group Policy Object and apply it to all users.

   c. Register the Microsoft Teams app as an Enterprise Application in Azure AD app registration.

   d. Publish the application using Microsoft Intune.

3. In preparation for the upgrade from Skype for Business to Microsoft Teams, you need to ensure all Skype for Business users have the Microsoft Teams client available on their Windows computers. How would you accomplish this?

   a. Add the Microsoft Teams client installer to your WSUS Server as an available update, and approve it for distribution.

   b. Download the Microsoft Teams client MSI and deploy it through a GPO.

   c. Log on to the Teams Admin Center, and publish the Microsoft Teams Client as an app.

   d. Log on to the Teams Admin Center, go to Org-wide Settings, and configure the Teams upgrade settings.

Skill 1.7: Monitor and analyze service usage

1. You want to use the Call Quality Dashboard to review call quality by location. When you log in, no locations have been defined. What should you do first?

    a. In the Teams Admin Center, run the Network Planner.

    b. In the Teams Admin Center, upload Reporting labels.

    c. In the Teams Admin Center, run Network Discovery.

    d. In the Teams Admin Center, access Network topology.

2. Following your upgrade to Microsoft Teams, management asks you for the number of users who are actively using Teams, and the number of active Teams channels. Where would you get this information?

    a. The Microsoft 365 User Activity Reports

    b. The Microsoft 365 Teams Usage Reports

    c. The Microsoft Teams User Activity Reports

    d. The Microsoft Teams Usage Reports

3. You need a helpdesk analyst to be able to review call quality metrics to triage support calls for poor audio for any user. What role should you add the helpdesk analyst to in order to provision them with the minimum privileges necessary to do this?

    a. Teams Service Administrator

    b. Teams User Administrator

    c. Teams Read-Only Administrator

    d. Teams Communications Support Engineer

Thought experiment answers

This section contains the solution to the thought experiment. Each answer explains why the answer choice is correct.

Skill 1.1: Upgrade from Skype for Business to Microsoft Teams

1. **d.** Use the Teams Admin Center to set "Download the Teams app in the background for Skype for Business users" to On.

    Skype for Business clients can automatically download the Microsoft Teams client without user prompting or interaction.

2. **c.** Set the coexistence mode to SfBWithTeamsCollab.

    SfBWithTeamsCollab keeps meetings and chat functionality within the Skype for Business client while enabling users to use Microsoft Teams for collaboration.

3. **a.** Confirm that the partner organization and you are both using Open Federation.

Just like Skype for Business Online, Microsoft Teams requires Open Federation and the use of SRV records to identify endpoints.

Skill 1.2: Plan and configure network settings for Microsoft Teams

1. **a.** Update the firewall to allow outbound traffic to UDP 3478-3481.

Streaming media including voice, video, and presentation sharing should use UDP to reduce overhead. The destination UDP ports used by Microsoft Teams are in the range of 3478-3481.

2. **b.** Use the Microsoft Teams Admin Center to enable QoS.

Only QoS enables networks to prioritize traffic based on the specific type.

3. **b.** Microsoft Teams Call Quality Dashboard.

CQD is the only tool of those listed that can show you historical packet loss.

Skill 1.3: Implement governance and lifecycle management for Microsoft Teams

1. **c.** In the Azure Portal, Groups, Expiration.

Office 365 Groups are the heart of a team, and expiration for them is controlled in the Azure portal.

2. **b.** Create a Sensitivity Label in the Security & Compliance Center and then edit the settings for the Team.

This is the correct way to accomplish this.

3. **a.** Azure Active Directory Access Reviews. Azure Active Directory Access Reviews are used to automate the process of reviewing access.

Skill 1.4: Configure and manage guest access

1. **c.** The Azure portal, Users, User settings, External users.

You can permit or block specific domains in the Azure portal, which then flows through to Microsoft Teams.

2. **d.** The Teams Admin Center, Org-wide Settings, Guest access.

Settings specific to how guests can use Teams are configured in the Org-wide Settings.

3. **a.** In the Azure portal, Identity Governance, Access reviews.

Guest access can be reviewed using Access Reviews.

Skill 1.5: Manage security and compliance

1. **b.** Place the user's mailbox on an in-place hold.

   1:1 chat messages are stored in the user's mailbox.

2. **a.** Teams Communications Administrator.

   This is the role with the least privilege that can accomplish this task.

3. **b.** In the Microsoft Teams Admin Center, under Org-wide Settings, modify Guest Access Settings.

   Restrictions on what guests can do within Microsoft Teams are configured in the Org-wide Settings.

Skill 1.6: Deploy and manage Microsoft Teams endpoints

1. **a.** Uninstall Microsoft Teams client from the VDI master image and then reinstall it.

   Nonpersistent VDIs are instantiated from a static image. To update the client, that image must be updated.

2. **d.** Publish the application using Microsoft Intune.

   To deploy an application automatically, Microsoft Intune can be used.

3. **d.** Log on to the Teams Admin Center, go to Org-wide Settings, and configure the Teams upgrade settings.

   You can deploy the Teams client to current Skype for Business users in this way.

Skill 1.7: Monitor and analyze service usage

1. **b.** In the Teams Admin Center, upload Reporting labels.

   Reporting labels are used to denote locations.

2. **d.** The Microsoft Teams Usage Reports.

   Microsoft Teams Usage Reports contain this information.

3. **d.** Teams Communications Support Engineer.

   This is the administrative role with the least privileges that is able to do this.

CHAPTER 2

Manage chat, calling, and meetings

In this chapter, we will look at the administrative tasks and policies associated with managing chat, calling, and meetings. These include enabling the services and configuring policies to control what can, and cannot, be done by end users. This chapter also contains almost everything to do with telephony. Although there are only four main skills in this section of the exam, each one has several topics included, and this section accounts for 30% to 35% of the exam content and may introduce concepts that are new to you if you're not managing telephony now. We will include URLs to helpful sites so that you can dig deeper if you want.

Skills covered in this chapter:

- Skill 2.1: Manage chat and collaboration experiences
- Skill 2.2: Manage meeting experiences
- Skill 2.3: Manage phone numbers
- Skill 2.4: Manage Phone System

Skill 2.1: Manage chat and collaboration experiences

This skill covers how to manage the chat and collaboration experiences for your users. This topic includes policies controlling what is and is not allowed across instant messaging, external collaboration, within channels, and integration with other services.

This skill covers how to:
- Configure messaging policies
- Manage external access
- Manage channels for a team
- Manage private channel creation
- Manage email integration
- Configure external access for SharePoint and OneDrive for Business
- Manage cloud file storage options for collaboration

Configure messaging policies

Messaging policies control what features are available to users of chat and messaging within channels. The Global (Org-wide default) policy will apply to all users unless you create and apply a different policy to others. Although many organizations may need only a single policy, Microsoft Teams is flexible so that you can have different policies based on job type or location.

Messaging policies control all aspects of chat messages, including whether or not users can even use chat, whether messages can be edited or deleted, and what can be included in messages. By default, all users have the Global (Org-wide default) policy applied to them, which enables them to use chat and most features. If your organization needs to be more restrictive, you can modify the Global (Org-wide default) policy. If you need to permit different things for different users, you can create multiple policies to meet your needs. Only one Messaging policy can be applied to any single user, though.

To create a new policy, do the following:

1. Log on to the TAC at *https://admin.teams.microsoft.com*.

2. In the left menu, select **Messaging policies**.

3. Click **+Add** to create a new Messaging policy.

4. Give the policy a name and a description, as shown in Figure 2-1.

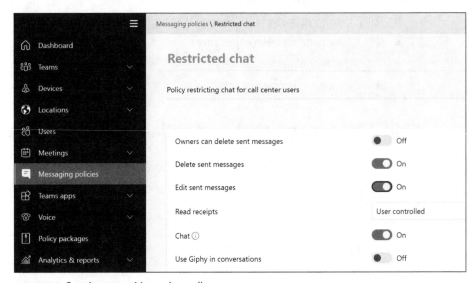

FIGURE 2-1 Creating a new Messaging policy

5. Modify the policy to meet your requirements. You may want to prevent users from deleting or editing messages once sent, turn off URL previews, or turn off Giphy or memes or stickers (but that takes all the fun out of things). Consider what you disable, because it will reduce the functionality for guest users. Figure 2-2 shows a more restrictive policy.

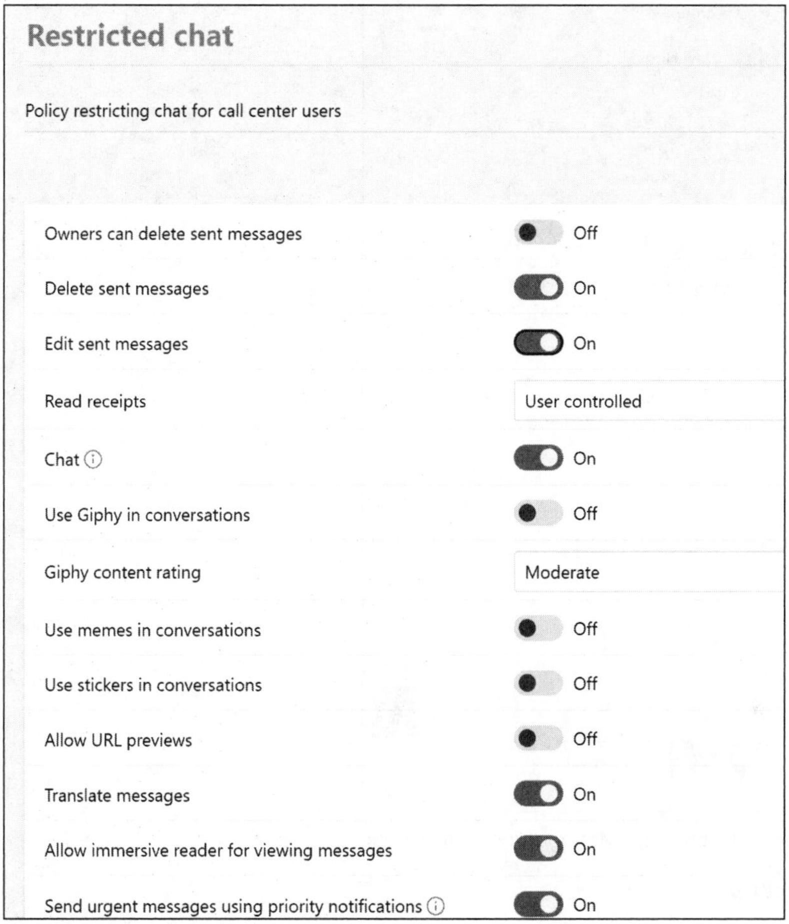

Restricted chat

Policy restricting chat for call center users

Owners can delete sent messages	Off
Delete sent messages	On
Edit sent messages	On
Read receipts	User controlled
Chat ⓘ	On
Use Giphy in conversations	Off
Giphy content rating	Moderate
Use memes in conversations	Off
Use stickers in conversations	Off
Allow URL previews	Off
Translate messages	On
Allow immersive reader for viewing messages	On
Send urgent messages using priority notifications ⓘ	On

FIGURE 2-2 A restrictive policy

6. When done, click **Save**.

You can assign Messaging policies directly to users, or you can assign them to groups. In either case, you can use the PowerShell cmdlet New-CsGroupPolicyAssignment, or you can use the TAC. To use the TAC to assign a Messaging policy to a group, follow these steps:

1. Select the **Group policy assignment** tab.

2. Select **+Add group**.

3. Enter the name of the group, or enough characters to enable the system to determine which group you intend, then select the search icon.

4. From the drop-down list, select the policy you wish to apply, as shown in Figure 2-3.

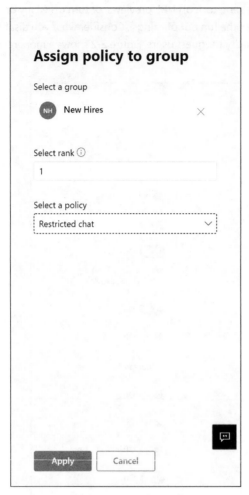

FIGURE 2-3 Applying a Messaging policy to a group

5. Select **Apply**.

NEED MORE REVIEW? **WHAT DOES EACH SETTING DO?**

To learn more about what each setting controls, see *https://docs.microsoft.com/en-US/ microsoftteams/messaging-policies-in-teams?WT.mc_id=TeamsAdminCenterCSH*.

Manage external access

In Skill 1.4 we reviewed how to configure and manage guest access. Here, we are going to look at managing external access, which is not the same, and is often referred to as *external federation.*

Guest access with Microsoft Teams controls what users who are invited to (and accept) access resources like Teams or Channels can do. Guest access users will have account objects that appear in your organization's Azure Active Directory. External access users are those in a federated organization who have not been explicitly invited as a guest and who do not have an object in the other organization's Azure AD.

External access controls how users in one organization can find, call, chat, and hold meetings with users in your organization. Table 2-1 compares what users in your organization can do with guests and with external access users by default.

TABLE 2-1 Your organization's user interactions with guest users vs. external access users

What your users can do with	Guest users	External access users
Interorganizational chat	Yes	Yes
Interorganizational calling	Yes	Yes
Interorganizational presence	Yes	Yes
Interorganizational search	Yes	No
Share files	Yes	No
View interorganizational Out of Office (OOF)	Yes	No
Interorganizational blocking	Yes	Yes

Table 2-2 provides a comparison of what users outside your organization can do within your tenant by default.

TABLE 2-2 What users outside of your organization can do

What users outside your organization can do	Guest users	External access users
Access Teams resources	Yes	No
Be added to a group chat	Yes	No
Be invited to a meeting	Yes	Yes
Make private calls	Yes	Yes
View the phone number for dial-in meeting participants	Yes	No
Use IP video	Yes	Yes
Use screen sharing	Yes	Yes
Use Meet Now	Yes	No
Edit sent messages	Yes	Yes
Delete sent messages	Yes	Yes
Use Giphy in conversation	Yes	Yes
Use memes in conversation	Yes	Yes
Use stickers in conversation	Yes	Yes
Presence is displayed	Yes	Yes
Use @mentions	Yes	Yes

The default settings for external access help facilitate fuller collaboration, but security policies may require that you restrict some of these settings. External access can be turned completely off or controlled by the Session Initiation Protocol (SIP) domain with permit and deny entries. You can also enable or disable external access with users of the consumer Skype service. To manage external access, do the following:

1. Log on to the TAC at *https://admin.teams.microsoft.com*.

2. In the left menu, expand **Org-wide settings** and then select **External access**.

3. If you wish to disable external access completely, set **Users can communicate with other Skype for Business and Teams users** to **Off**.

4. If you wish to only disable external access with users of the Skype consumer service, set **Users can communicate with Skype users** to **Off**.

5. To either explicitly permit or explicitly deny specific domains, select **+Add a domain**.

6. Add the specific domain DNS name and specify whether to allow or deny it, as shown in Figure 2-4.

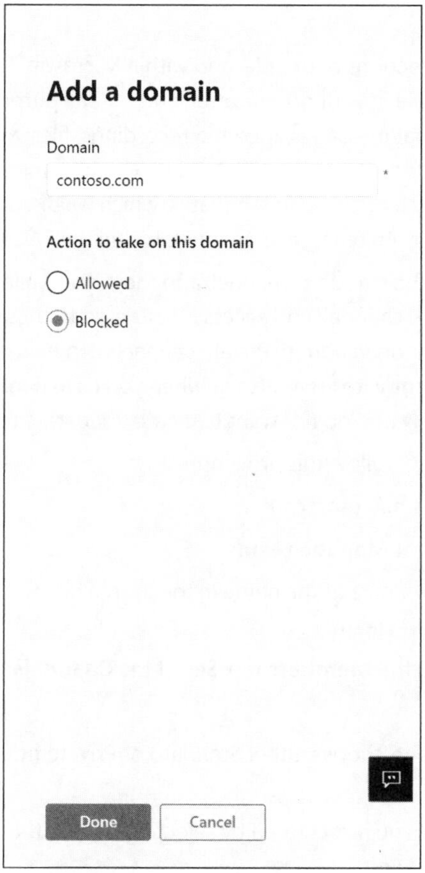

FIGURE 2-4 Blocking a SIP domain

7. Select **Done**.

> **REAL WORLD** **YOU CAN ADD BOTH, BUT DON'T.**
>
> Pay attention to the note in the TAC about blocking and allowing. By default, external access is allowed with ALL domains if it is turned on. If you add an ALLOW entry, then that is allowed and ALL others are implicitly blocked. If you add a BLOCK entry, then that domain is blocked but ALL others are implicitly allowed. You can add both BLOCK and ALLOW, but don't. Also remember that external access is a two-way street. If you are explicitly allowing a partner domain, and they have explicit ALLOW entries but forget to include your domain, external access will not work. If you are explicitly allowing them but they are either explicitly or implicitly denying you, external access will not work. And don't forget the DNS SRV records for your domain. If the other domain is either a Skype for Business organization or is in hybrid, the DNS SRV records for your domain are required, even if all your users are 100% in Teams.

Manage channels for a team

Teams are, at their most fundamental level, collections of people, and within Microsoft Teams, you can create a team for any grouping of people in your organization and for any purpose. Channels exist within a team and can include chat messages, meeting recordings, files, and other tools. Every team has a General channel (that cannot be deleted), and team owners can create other channels at need, either from scratch or by using templates, which we discussed in Chapter 1. Admins can also create and manage both teams and channels within the TAC.

There are two kinds of channels. The first is the standard channel, and these are available to all members of a team. The second is the private channel, and access is restricted to those who are explicitly added to that channel by an owner or an admin. Private channels can be useful within a larger team if you want to have a more private area, such as when you have guests in a team but need an area that is for employees only and do not want to create a separate team.

To manage channels for a team using the TAC, follow this procedure:

1. Log on to the TAC at *https://admin.teams.microsoft.com*.
2. In the left menu, expand **Teams** and select **Manage teams**.
3. Scroll down the list of your teams, or enter part of the name in the Search box to find your team, and then select the name of the team.
4. You can see the list of team members on the **Members** tab. Select the **Channels** tab.
5. To create a new channel, select **+Add**.
6. Name the channel, enter a description, and choose either Standard or Private from the type drop-down list. Then select **Apply**.
7. In the list of channels, select the channel you just created by selecting next to the name so that a check mark appears, then select **Edit**.
8. In this window, you can change the name and the description. You cannot change between private and public. If you make any changes, select **Apply** to save them.
9. While all members of a team have access to public channels, you must explicitly add team members to private channels. To do this, select the name of the private channel.
10. In this window, select **+Add** to add new members. Remember that only existing members of the team can be assigned to a private channel. If you do not see a user you wish to add, go back to the team and ensure they are a member.
11. When finished, select **Apply**.

Channels can also be managed by a team owner in the Teams app or Teams web app. To do so:

1. Log on to Microsoft Teams.
2. On the Teams tab, browse down to your team, or use Search and select your team.
3. Select the ellipsis button (or right-click the team), and you will see options for managing the team, including creating new channels.
4. To manage an existing channel, select the ellipsis button (or right-click the channel) and you will see options for managing the channel, as shown in Figure 2-5.

FIGURE 2-5 Managing a channel; note the padlock icon, which indicates this is a private channel

5. Just as in the TAC, you can edit the properties of a channel or add new members to a private channel.

There are limitations to private channels you should consider when using them. They do not support all the connectors and tabs and apps that public channels do. They are not copied to a new team if you create one from an existing team that has private channels. Notifications for activities in private channels are not included in missed activity emails. And perhaps most importantly, at present retention policies are not supported. Messages sent to members of private channels are stored in the members' mailboxes, rather than the team's mailbox. You can, of course, place retention on users' mailboxes and run eDiscovery searches against user mailboxes. But if your organization requires retention on the team content and not on the members, you may need to create a private team, rather than a private channel within an existing team, to meet your needs. One other point of note to be clear on: unlike the team itself, once created, a channel cannot be changed from Standard to Private or vice versa. Another reason to be very deliberate when creating a private channel!

Manage private channel creation

By default, just as all users can create teams, any owner of a team can create private channels with the teams they own. You can restrict this if necessary by creating a Teams policy to restrict the ability to create private channels and applying it to users. As an admin, you can then create private channels for teams that require them and meet whatever internal guidelines you have in place for this. To restrict private channel creation for your entire organization, do the following:

1. Log on to the TAC at *https://admin.teams.microsoft.com*.

2. In the left menu, expand **Teams**, and select **Teams policies**.

3. Select the **Global (Org-wide default)** policy and then select **Edit**.

4. Set the **Create private channels** switch to **Off**, as shown in Figure 2-6.

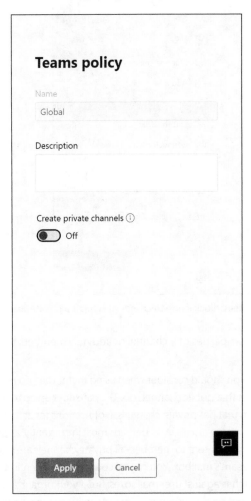

FIGURE 2-6 The global policy preventing the creation of private channels

5. Select **Apply**.

You can create additional Teams policies and assign them to specific users if you need some users to be able to create private channels and prevent others from doing so.

> **REAL WORLD** **TEAMS IS CONSTANTLY INNOVATING**
>
> The next big thing coming to Microsoft Teams is Microsoft Teams Connect. Also known as Shared Channels, Microsoft Teams Connect approaches the need to have external collaboration from the opposite direction of private channels by letting you have a team without external members, and create a channel within that team to which you can invite external collaborators directly, without giving them access to anything else in the team. Better still, you won't have to switch tenants to access a Microsoft Teams Connect channel where you are a guest, making cross-org collaboration even easier. Keep an eye open for more on this feature and expect it to be covered in a future revision of this exam.

Manage email integration

By default, each team, and each channel within a team, are assigned an email address that can accept mail. Email sent to the team address will appear in the General channel, as will email sent to the General channel address, whereas email sent to any other channel will appear in the appropriate channel. This can be used for including teams or channels in email blasts, to subscribe to RSS feeds, for SMTP-based alerts, and more. You can restrict email access on an organizational level, on a team level, and at a channel level if necessary.

Email addresses are, by default, assigned to every channel in a team from the tenant routing domain and region, such as 0c9188db.M365x397752.onmicrosoft.com@amer.teams.ms. The first eight characters uniquely identify the team and channel, then the tenant name that was created when the tenant was first set up, then the @ sign, then the regional teams domain. In the earlier case, the tenant name is M365x397752.onmicrosoft.com and it was created in the North American (amer) region. Once you add and verify a custom domain in your tenant and set its purpose for email, email addresses will be user-friendlier and assigned in the default SMTP domain. You can assign a different SMTP address if you prefer.

To manage email integration at the organizational level, do the following:

1. Log on to the TAC at *https://admin.teams.microsoft.com*.
2. In the left menu, expand **Org-wide settings**, then select **Teams settings**.
3. Scroll down to **Email integration**.
4. You can turn off email integration by setting **Allow users to send emails to channel email address** to **Off**, or you can restrict what SMTP domains can send email to teams, as shown in Figure 2-7.

FIGURE 2-7 The Org-wide settings for email integration

5. When you are done making changes, scroll down to the bottom of the Teams settings panel and select **Save**.

To change the address of a team, do the following:

1. As an Exchange admin or recipient admin, log on to the Exchange admin center at *https://admin.exchange.microsoft.com*.

2. Expand **Recipients** and then select **Groups**.

3. Find the Office 365 Group that corresponds to the team you wish to update.

4. Select the group.

5. Details of the group will be shown in a pop-up window. In the Email addresses section, select **Edit**.

6. You can edit the primary email address, or add one or more aliases and then set an alias as the primary, as shown in Figure 2-8.

FIGURE 2-8 Editing the email address for an Office 365 Group

7. When done, select **Save changes**.

Configure external access for SharePoint and OneDrive for Business

As you know by now, Microsoft Teams is heavily dependent on SharePoint and One-Drive for Business. Each team has an associated SharePoint site. Each public channel within a team has an associated folder. Ad hoc sharing uses OneDrive for Business. Both fall under compliance and retention policies set at the organizational level to facilitate administration.

As teams may have external guest members, how SharePoint and OneDrive for Business are configured for external access can have a direct impact on using Teams with external guests. Microsoft Teams uses the settings from SharePoint and OneDrive for Business that control sharing of files, including the defaults when sharing. If a team wants to include external users, but the SharePoint admin has blocked external sharing, the more restrictive setting will take precedence and could lead to unexpected results for the team owner. It's recommended that you use a more open approach to sharing within SharePoint and then implement more restrictive settings on sites that specifically hold more sensitive information, and the Microsoft Teams admin(s) and the SharePoint admin(s) work together to ensure that all settings deployed support the business need and meet specific company policies.

To set Sharing permissions at the organizatonal level, which will then apply to teams, do the following:

1. Log on to the SharePoint admin center at *https://tenantname-admin.sharepoint.com*.

2. In the left menu, expand **Policies** and select **Sharing**.

3. In the **External sharing** section, select the **More external sharing settings** link to see all the options, and then set the level of permissions that meets the organization's broadest requirements. It is also possible, through the Active Sites page in the SharePoint admin center, as well as through PowerShell, to set more granular options for external sharing at the site level. An example of this would be to allow external sharing for team sites for collaboration while blocking the ability to share content from a corporate intranet site. Note that you can also restrict sharing to only specific domains, such as partner domains, if desired, and this can also be configured granularly. Figure 2-9 shows the options for this.

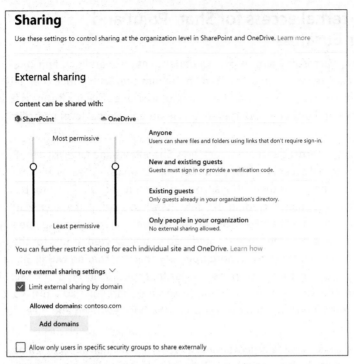

FIGURE 2-9 External sharing settings for SharePoint and OneDrive for Business

4. Depending on the desired sharing posture for your organization, you can set default settings for sharing file and folder links, as shown in Figure 2-10. Note that these settings can be changed by the user up to the most permissive external sharing settings applied as previously discussed.

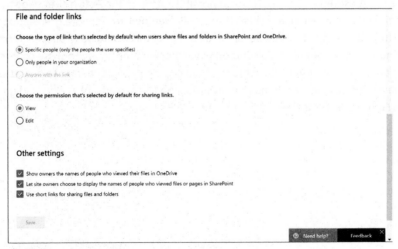

FIGURE 2-10 Editing the default file and folder link settings

5. When you are finished making changes, select **Save**.

Manage cloud file storage options for collaboration

Microsoft Teams is built to utilize SharePoint and OneDrive for Business for cloud file storage, but it can also integrate with several third-party storage services. This is useful for organizations that have already deployed competing solutions, including Box and DropBox, among others. Teams admins can control which services are available globally in Teams settings. The default is to permit all available, but you may wish to disable one or all to meet corporate compliance or security requirements. To manage which cloud file storage options are available, do the following:

1. Log on to the TAC at *https://admin.teams.microsoft.com*.

2. In the left menu, expand **Org-wide settings** and then select **Teams settings**.

3. Disable any of the third-party solutions you do not want users to access by setting the switch to **Off**, as shown in Figure 2-11.

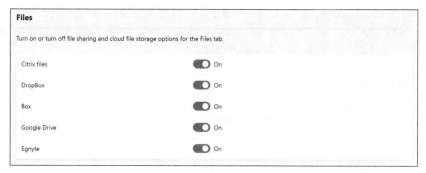

FIGURE 2-11 Editing the default third-party file sharing services available

4. Scroll down to the bottom of the window and select **Save**.

Skill 2.2: Manage meeting experiences

Where would work be without meetings? Don't answer that. Instead, consider that a significant amount of your users' time will be spent attending meetings, so you want to ensure that they have the best technical experience possible. As a Teams administrator, you can control a number of the settings that will directly impact what can, and cannot, be done within meetings.

> **This skill covers how to:**
> - Configure meeting settings
> - Create and manage meeting policies
> - Configure settings for live events
> - Create and manage policies for live events
> - Configure conference bridge settings

Configure meeting settings

Meeting settings control high-level aspects of all meetings, including whether or not anonymous users can attend, as well as the links that are included within a meeting invitation. You may want to point attendees to your own internal URLs or include your corporate logo in meeting invites. You can also, if necessary, control network settings for meetings, including quality of service (QoS) and the port ranges used.

To configure meeting settings, do the following:

1. Log on to the TAC at *https://admin.teams.microsoft.com*.

2. In the left menu, expand **Meetings** and select **Meeting settings**.

3. In **Meeting settings**, first determine whether or not you wish to permit anonymous users, and whether or not they can interact with apps (like the Whiteboard) in meetings.

4. You can then customize the contents of meeting invites to include your company logo, links to your legal and/or help URL, and any text you want to include in the footer, as shown in Figure 2-12. Note that links must be HTTPS.

FIGURE 2-12 Editing the meeting settings

5. Once you have the URLs entered, you can select **Preview invite** to see what your meeting invite will look like, as shown in Figure 2-13.

   If necessary, you can then scroll down to enable QoS and to change the port ranges used for Teams meetings, as shown in Figure 2-14.

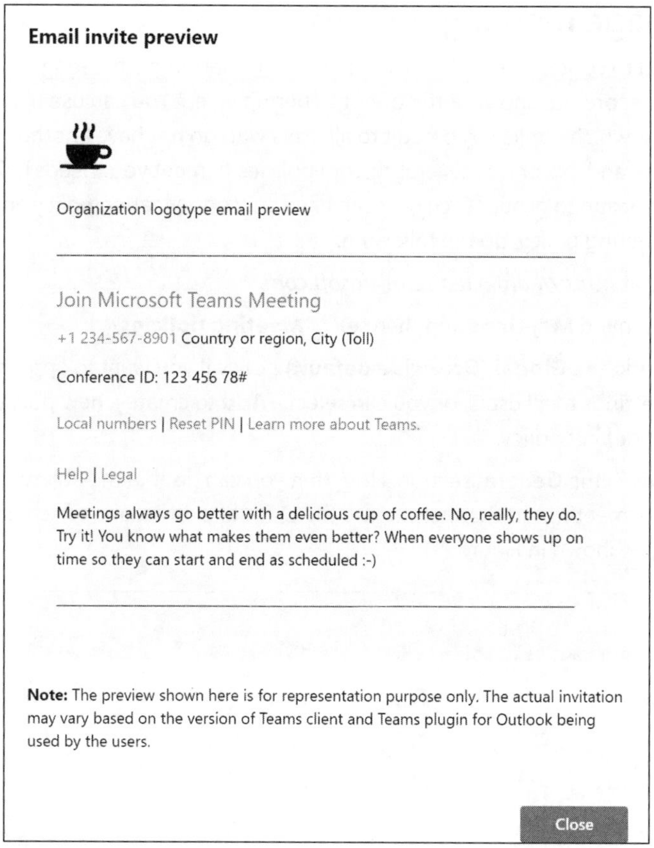

Email invite preview

Organization logotype email preview

_____

Join Microsoft Teams Meeting

+1 234-567-8901 **Country or region, City (Toll)**

Conference ID: 123 456 78#

Local numbers | Reset PIN | Learn more about Teams.

Help | Legal

Meetings always go better with a delicious cup of coffee. No, really, they do.
Try it! You know what makes them even better? When everyone shows up on
time so they can start and end as scheduled :-)

_____

Note: The preview shown here is for representation purpose only. The actual invitation
may vary based on the version of Teams client and Teams plugin for Outlook being
used by the users.

Close

FIGURE 2-13 A preview of a meeting invite

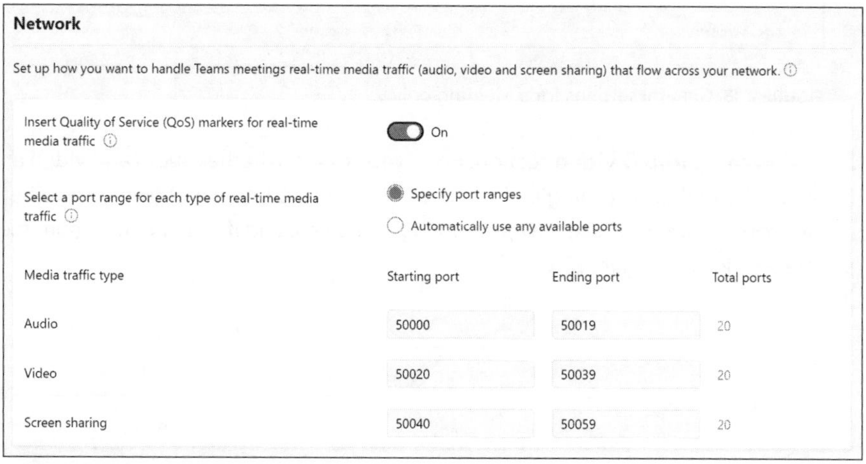

Network

Set up how you want to handle Teams meetings real-time media traffic (audio, video and screen sharing) that flow across your network. ⓘ

Insert Quality of Service (QoS) markers for real-time
media traffic ⓘ   On

Select a port range for each type of real-time media   ⦿ Specify port ranges
traffic ⓘ
                                                              ◯ Automatically use any available ports

Media traffic type	Starting port	Ending port	Total ports
Audio	50000	50019	20
Video	50020	50039	20
Screen sharing	50040	50059	20

FIGURE 2-14 Network settings

6. Select **Save** when done.

Create and manage meeting policies

Meeting policies are used to control the features available when users join a meeting, including things like transcription, recording, and whether or not to permit video. You can use the Global (Org-wide Default) policy, which applies by default to all users who do not have another policy applied. Or you can create and use one of several custom policies to meet your needs if they vary from user to user or group to group. Each user can have only one Meeting policy applied to them. To manage a Meeting policy, do the following:

1. Log on to the TAC at *https://admin.teams.microsoft.com*.

2. In the left menu, expand **Meetings** and then select **Meeting policies**.

3. You can select to edit the **Global (Org-wide default)** policy if you want to apply a consistent group of settings to all users, or you can select **+Add** to create a new policy. Here we will look at the default policy.

4. Review the settings in the **General** section. Note that you can disable the ability to meet now or to schedule meetings in channels, to use the Outlook add-in, and to schedule private meetings, as shown in Figure 2-15.

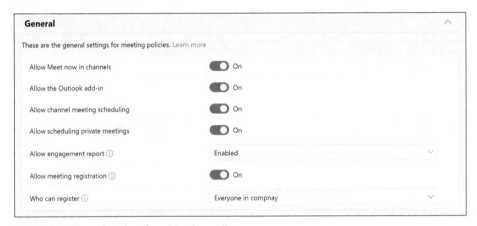

FIGURE 2-15 General settings for a Meeting policy

5. Review the **Audio & video** section. Here, you control whether audio and video are allowed, whether recording is allowed, whether transcription is allowed, and whether Network Device Interface (NDI) streaming is allowed, and if it is, the maximum media bit rate, as shown in Figure 2-16.

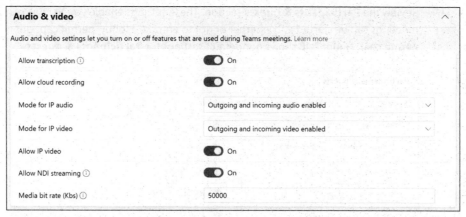

FIGURE 2-16 Audio and video settings

6. Review the **Content sharing** section. Here, you control whether screen sharing is permitted or restricted to a single app, whether others can request control, if PowerPoint sharing is permitted, if whiteboard is permitted, if notes are permitted, and if video filters are permitted. If you are concerned about sharing sensitive or proprietary information on a Teams meeting, you may wish to disable sharing content sharing completely, as shown in Figure 2-17.

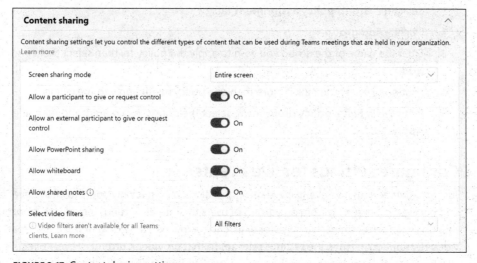

FIGURE 2-17 Content sharing settings

7. Review the **Participants & guests** section. These settings enable you to control how meetings can be started and whether or not to enforce a lobby, permit captions, and permit chat. Figure 2-18 shows nondefault settings for **Participants & guests**.

FIGURE 2-18 Participants and guests settings

8. If you made any changes to the **Global (Org-wide default)** policy, select **Save**.

If you created a new policy and wish to apply it to users, do the following:

1. Select the **Group policy assignment** tab.
2. Select **+Add group**.
3. Enter the name of the group you wish to apply the policy to, then select them and select **Add**.
4. (Optional) Select the rank if more than one policy might apply to the group.
5. From the **Select a policy** drop-down, select the policy you created, and then select **Apply**.

Configure settings for live events

Just as with meetings, live events have settings that should uniformly apply to all live events and policies that may vary from one group of users to another. Settings include a support URL that users can select to reach a page for assistance, and if you are going to use a third-party video distribution partner, the settings relevant to that provider. Currently, Hive, Kollective, and Riverbed are supported with Microsoft Teams live events and have their own costs that are between you and the provider. These can reduce the impact to your network when many users want to view a live event from the same location, but they are not required. To configure these settings, follow these steps:

1. Log on to the TAC at *https://admin.teams.microsoft.com*.
2. In the left menu, expand **Meetings** and then select **Live event settings**.
3. Enter the custom URL for support, if available.

4. If using a video distribution partner, select that partner from the **SDN provider name** drop-down list, and then enter the API key or license key and the URL provided by the SDN partner.

Create and manage policies for live events

Live event policies control who can schedule a live event, as well as some other settings. As with other policies, you can have a single global policy that applies to all, or you can create multiple policies and apply them to different groups of users. To do this, follow these steps:

1. Log on to the TAC at *https://admin.teams.microsoft.com*.

2. In the left menu, expand **Meetings** and then select **Live events policies**.

3. The **Global (Org-wide default)** policy will apply to everyone who does not have another policy applied. That policy permits live events and allows transcription and recording, as shown in Figure 2-19.

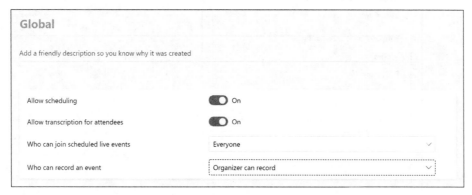

FIGURE 2-19 Global live event settings

4. If you need to make changes, make sure to select **Save** when done.

5. Select **+Add** to create a new policy with the settings you desire, and select **Save** when done.

6. Select the **Group policy assignment** tab.

7. Select **+Add group**, search for and select the group of users to which you wish to apply the policy, select the rank (optional), and then select the policy from the drop-down list.

8. Finally, select **Apply**.

Configure conference bridge settings

Conference bridges are used when people wish to dial a telephone number to participate in the audio portion of a meeting. Conference bridges are available for any user who schedules a meeting and has an appropriate audio-conferencing license. There are both flat monthly fee and per-minute options available for customers in most locations, as well as local numbers in many locations. There are shared numbers that are available to all customers, or you can obtain numbers at an additional charge for your exclusive use You can accept the default, or configure bridge settings to meet your organization's needs. To do this, follow these steps:

1. Log on to the TAC at *https://admin.teams.microsoft.com*.

2. In the left menu, expand **Meetings**, and then select **Conference bridges**.

3. If you have your own toll or toll-free number you wish to use, you can select **+Add** to add them.

4. To change bridge settings, select **Bridge settings**.

5. You can specify whether or not to notify when someone joins a conference bridge with either a tone or an announcement of their name if they used their PIN to authenticate, or the phone number from which they dialed in if they did not, as shown in Figure 2-20.

FIGURE 2-20 Bridge settings

6. If you made any changes, select **Apply** to exit.

7. You can choose a default number to be included in meeting invites by finding one of the shared numbers in the list, and then selecting it and selecting **Set as default**. That number will be included in the meeting invites sent by users who do not have a more specific number configured for their user in their audio-conferencing configuration.

Skill 2.3: Manage phone numbers

Microsoft Teams provides customers with options for a complete voice solution. Microsoft can serve as your telephone company in many regions using a calling plan, or you can choose a local telco provider and utilize direct routing. Some organizations may use both approaches, depending on where they operate or what specific needs they have. Whichever approach you choose, Microsoft Teams provides a rich set of calling features and both soft-phone capabilities as well as the ability to integrate with physical devices.

This skill covers how to:

- Recommend a PSTN connectivity solution based on specific business requirements
- Order phone numbers
- Manage service numbers
- Add, change, or remove an emergency address for your organization
- Assign, change, or remove a phone number for a user
- Manage voice and audio-conferencing settings for users
- Configure dynamic emergency policies

Recommend a PSTN connectivity solution based on specific business requirements

When planning a Teams Voice solution, you need to determine whether Microsoft can meet all of your organization's needs, in all of your organization's locations, or if you will need to include services from one or more telephony providers. Phone System is Microsoft's technology that provides a complete call control and private branch exchange (PBX) solution for customers. It offers all the major capabilities most customers will need, including the following:

- Call control
- PBX
- Auto attendants
- Call queues
- Cloud voicemail
- Caller ID
- Music on hold
- Select-to-call
- Call forwarding and simultaneous ring
- Presence-based call routing
- VoIP calls with federated partners

And more. The only thing missing is connectivity to the public switched telephone network (PSTN.) If you want to connect your voice solution to the PSTN, you need to choose one or more solutions that meet your organization's needs. In a growing number of countries, Microsoft is a telephony provider and offers Phone System with Calling Plans that include direct inward dialing (DID) and outbound calling with both local and long distance. With Phone System available in a growing number of countries, many customers will find that it meets all their needs.

However, if your organization requires local telephone services in countries where Microsoft is not (currently) a telecom provider, you have a larger deployment that may include legacy analog components, and/or you have existing telecom contracts with one or more carriers, you may choose to deploy Phone System with your own PSTN carrier, commonly called *direct routing*. These are not mutually exclusive solutions, and you may have both to support your organization in different locations.

If your organization meets the following criteria:

- Microsoft offers Calling Plans in your region.
- You do not need to retain your existing PSTN carrier.
- You do not have an existing deployment of analog or other legacy telephony gear.
- You want to use Microsoft to access PSTN.

then Phone System With Calling Plan is a good solution for your organization. If your organization has the following requirements:

- You need to retain your existing PSTN carrier.
- You need to interoperate with third-party PBXs and/or legacy or analog equipment.
- You have or are willing to deploy a supported session border controller (SBC) solution.

then direct routing is a good solution for your organization.

EXAM TIP

This overview is a good introduction to the criteria for recommending a PSTN connectivity solution and may cover the broad strokes of the exam, but there is a lot more that goes into this. You should review the content starting at *https://docs.microsoft.com/en-us/microsoftteams/ cloud-voice-landing-page* and linked from there to get a better feel for the options, differences, pros, and cons of each approach.

NOTE   NEW REGIONS ARE ADDED REGULARLY

The regions where Microsoft can offer Calling Plans is growing constantly. You always want to check the documentation to see if regions in which you operate have been added. See *https://docs.microsoft.com/en-us/microsoftteams/country-and-region-availability-for-audio-conferencing-and-calling-plans/country-and-region-availability-for-audio-conferencing-and-calling-plans* and check back frequently if a region your organization requires is not currently listed.

Order phone numbers

For your users to be reached by other users on the PSTN, they need telephone numbers. When Microsoft is your telco because you are using Phone System with Calling Plans, Microsoft can provide you telephone numbers or you can port existing numbers you already have from another provider.

Greenfield deployments and expansions where existing service is not already deployed can easily request new phone numbers from Microsoft in any region where Microsoft offers calling. If you are replacing your existing service with Microsoft but want to keep your existing phone numbers (since they are probably well known, on business cards and websites, and in customers' speed dials) porting your existing numbers from your original telco to Microsoft enables you to maintain your numbers. In many locations, you can order new phone numbers directly through the TAC.

To order new phone numbers, do the following:

1. Log on to the TAC at *https://admin.teams.microsoft.com*.

2. In the left menu, expand **Voice** and then select **Phone numbers**.

3. You will see existing phone numbers already in your tenant, and you can filter or sort by Unassigned if you just need to find a number to assign a user. To order new phone numbers, select **+Add**.

4. Enter an order name and a friendly description to help you keep track of the order.

5. For **Location and quantity**, first select the country or region from the drop-down list.

6. Select the **Number type** from the next drop-down list, as shown in Figure 2-21.

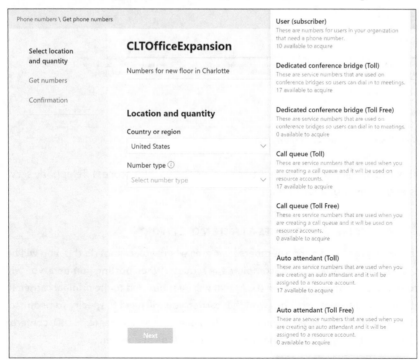

FIGURE 2-21 Options for number type

7. Enter the quantity of telephone numbers you need, up to the maximum available to you.

8. To choose a specific region or area code, either enter the city name, select the location, and then select the area code, or simply select the **Search by area code** radio button and then enter the area code. Then select **Next**.

9. Review the number(s) offered, and if they are acceptable, select **Place order**. Note that you only have 10 minutes to complete this, or you will have to start over.

10. Select **Finish**.

It may take a few moments before the new number appears in your phone numbers inventory. Once it does, it can be assigned as appropriate. Remember that you may need to assign a license before you can assign a phone number. If you need more than one type of number, such as User and Call queue, repeat the process for each type of number.

To port existing numbers from a carrier to Microsoft, you can select the **Port** button and complete the process. You are guided through it in the TAC, as shown in Figure 2-22.

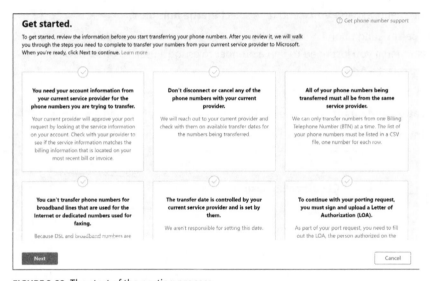

FIGURE 2-22 The start of the porting process

You should allow at least two weeks to complete the porting process. Telephony services will transfer over without interruption.

> **REAL WORLD SOMETIMES IT TAKES A LITTLE MORE EFFORT**
>
> If you are trying to obtain phone numbers in an area where you cannot do this, you will be able to download an order form to complete the request. When porting numbers, you will need to sign a letter of authorization (LOA) that will be submitted to the original carrier. If you are not authorized to make changes with that carrier, you will need to specify someone to sign that letter. Also note that when porting more than one type of number (e.g., DID, conference bridge), you must complete a porting request for each type of number.

Manage service numbers

Service numbers include both toll and toll-free numbers, which can be used for audio-conferencing. After you obtain service numbers, you need to assign each number to an audio-conferencing bridge, change the default number for your conference bridge, and then change the conference bridge information that is included in invites. You can also update existing meeting invites if desired, but remember that the Meeting Migration Service (covered in Skill 1-1) has a number of limitations. You may just want to let attrition age out the shared number and use the new service number for all meetings going forward. To assign a new service number to an audio-conferencing bridge, do the following:

1. Log on to the TAC at *https://admin.teams.microsoft.com.*
2. In the left menu, expand **Voice** and then select **Phone numbers.**
3. Select the service number you want to assign and select **Edit.**
4. From the **Assigned to** drop-down list, select **Conference bridge**, as shown in Figure 2-23.

FIGURE 2-23 Assigning a service number to a conference bridge

5. Select **Apply**.

6. Expand **Meetings** and select **Conference bridges**.

7. Sort on type so that Dedicated is listed first, then select the service number that you added earlier.

8. Select **Set as default**.

To change the default audio-conferencing number for a single user:

1. Log on to the TAC at *https://admin.teams.microsoft.com*.

2. In the left menu, select **Users** and then select the user you wish to modify.

3. The user page will open. Scroll down to the **Audio conferencing** section and select **Edit**.

4. Find the number you wish to use and select it, as shown in Figure 2-24.

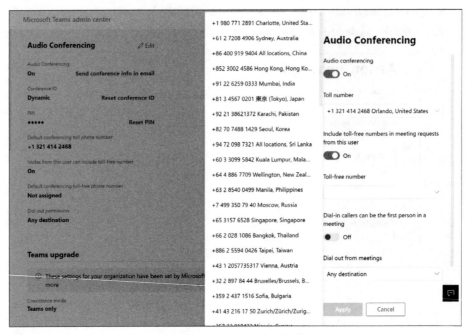

FIGURE 2-24 Assigning a service number to a conference bridge for a user

5. Select **Apply**.

> **NOTE USE POWERSHELL TO SCALE**
>
> If you need to assign a new dedicated conference number to several users, you want to use the PowerShell cmdlet Set-CsOnlineDialInConferencingUserDefaultNumber. See *https://docs. microsoft.com/en-us/powershell/module/skype/set-csonlinedialinconferencinguserdefaultnum ber?view=skype-ps* for more on that.

Add, change, or remove an emergency address for your organization

Microsoft Teams supports emergency calling to public authorities and can also notify organization contacts whenever a user calls an emergency services number such as 911 in the United States, and 999 elsewhere. Users can be assigned to locations so that, when they make an emergency call, their location information can be shared with emergency services. Emergency addresses are static and appropriate for users with phones whose location does not change. For a more mobile workforce, see "Configure dynamic emergency policies" later in this chapter.

To work with emergency addresses in your organization, do the following:

1. Log on to the TAC at *https://admin.teams.microsoft.com*.

2. In the left menu, expand **Locations** and select **Emergency addresses**.

3. In the **Emergency addresses** pane, select **+Add**.

4. Enter a name for the location, select the country or region, and complete the required information. Note that when entering latitude and longitude, you must use decimal values.

5. When done, select **Save**.

   If you wish to work with multiple locations, you can use the PowerShell cmdlets **New-CsOnlineLisCivicAddress**, **Set-CsOnlineLisCivicAddress**, and **Remove-CsOnlineLisCivicAddress**.

   You can then assign the location to telephone numbers in use for users with a fixed location. To do this:

1. Expand **Voice** and select **Phone numbers**.

2. Select the phone number you want to assign to a location, and select **Edit**.

3. In the **Assign/unassign** pane, scroll down to **Emergency location** and search for the location, using city, description, or place. Select the appropriate location and then select **Apply**.

You can also remove or change a location for a user in the same location. If you want to assign a location to multiple users, you should use the PowerShell cmdlet Set-CsOnlineVoiceUser.

NEED MORE REVIEW? **EMERGENCY LOCATIONS ARE KEY**

See *https://docs.microsoft.com/en-us/microsoftteams/what-are-emergency-locations-addresses-and-call-routing* for more information on this topic.

Based on the user's network location, Teams can automatically route the call to the appropriate public safety answering point (PSAP) and pass the caller's physical location to the dispatcher so that emergency responders can be directed to the location where they are needed.

For this to work, the Teams administrator must configure network locations and the Location Information Service (LIS) in the TAC with the physical addresses (and perhaps more detail, like floor or office) for users. If a user initiates an emergency call using Teams and is on a network without location information, the call is connected through the default calling path and the caller must provide their location to the PSAP dispatcher. To identify where a user is located, you can use an IP subnet, a switch port, a wireless access point, or a switch.

To configure dynamic emergency policies, do the following:

1. Log on to the TAC at *https://admin.teams.microsoft.com*.
2. In the left menu, expand **Locations**, and select **Networks & locations**.
3. You can add subnets, Wi-Fi access points, switches, or switch ports. On the **Subnets** tab, select **+Add**.
4. Enter the subnet information and associate it with the emergency location.
5. When finished, select **Apply**.

Assign, change, or remove a phone number for a user

Managing telephone numbers can include assigning a phone number to a user, changing it if necessary, and then removing it if the user no longer needs it. These tasks can be accomplished in the TAC or with PowerShell. To use the TAC, do the following:

1. Log on to the TAC at *https://admin.teams.microsoft.com*.
2. In the left menu, expand **Voice** and select **Phone numbers**.
3. Select a phone number, and then select **Edit**.
4. If you selected an unassigned number, enter enough in the **Search by display or username** field to find the user to which you want to assign the number. Select the user and select **Assign**, as shown in Figure 2-25.

FIGURE 2-25 Assigning a telephone number to a user

5. Search for and assign the appropriate **Emergency location**.
6. Select **Apply** to finish.

You can repeat the process to remove a number or to change to a different number. Remember that to assign a telephone number to a user, the number must be unassigned, and the user must have a phone system license associated with them and perhaps a calling plan license depending on whether or not direct routing is involved.

Manage voice and audio-conferencing settings for users

Users with an audio-conferencing license can send out meeting invites that include a dial-in number for users who want to participate in the audio portion of a meeting using the PSTN. Once licensed, users' meeting invites will include one or more dial-in numbers and a meeting conference ID, and they will have an audio-conferencing PIN they can use to start a meeting if they need to dial in. Users' audio-conferencing bridges include several settings as well, including entry and exit notifications. Once a license is assigned, all of these can be set in the TAC or through PowerShell.

To assign an Audio Conferencing license, do the following:

1. Log on to the Microsoft 365 Admin portal at *https://admin.microsoft.com*.
2. In the left menu, expand **Users** and then select **Active users**.
3. Select the user or users to which you wish to assign an audio-conferencing license or a plan license that includes audio-conferencing and assign the appropriate license.
4. Log on to the TAC at *https://admin.teams.microsoft.com*.
5. In the left menu, expand **Users** and select the user you wish to manage.
6. On the **Account** tab, scroll down to **Audio conferencing**.
7. By default, conferencing information will automatically be sent to the user in email if it changes, conference IDs are set dynamically, and the user's PIN is set at random. You can select any of these settings to change/reset them.
8. To set conferencing telephone numbers and control other settings, select **Edit**.
9. You can disable audio-conferencing, select the toll (or toll-free if available) number to include in an invite, allow dial-in callers to start a meeting, and control dial-out settings, as shown in Figure 2-26.

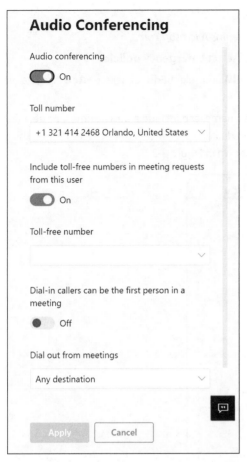

Audio Conferencing

Audio conferencing

On

Toll number

+1 321 414 2468 Orlando, United States

Include toll-free numbers in meeting requests from this user

On

Toll-free number

Dial-in callers can be the first person in a meeting

Off

Dial out from meetings

Any destination

Apply   Cancel

FIGURE 2-26 Setting audio-conferencing settings for a user

10. If you make any changes, select **Apply** to save them.

Configure dynamic emergency policies

Emergency calling policies control dynamic emergency calling and enable local security or other personnel to be added to a call when a user calls emergency services. A Global (Org-wide default) policy can apply to all users, or you can create additional policies to apply to specific locations. Options include notification, conferencing in on mute, and conferencing in unmuted, and enable you to ensure local responders are aware of an emergency call when it is made, and not to require users to call the on-premises responders before or after calling emergency services.

To configure this policy, do the following:

1. Log on to the TAC at *https://admin.teams.microsoft.com*.

2. In the left menu, expand **Voice** and select **Emergency policies**.

3. Select the **Global (Org-wide default)** and select **Edit**, or select **+Add** create a new policy.

4. Emergency calling policies require a name, can include a description, a notification mode, and either a PSTN number to dial or a user/group to notify. Configure the policy to meet your location's needs, as shown in Figure 2-27.

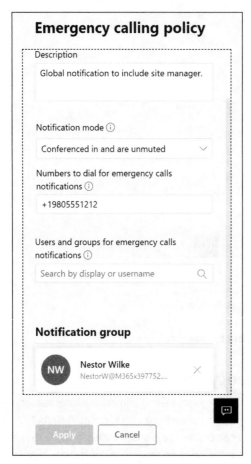

FIGURE 2-27 Setting an emergency calling policy

5. When finished, select **Apply**.

Skill 2.4: Manage Phone System

Teams admins have many tasks that they may have to perform to manage the phone system for their organization. Most are more of a setup than a daily or repeating task, unless the organization is experiencing significant growth or going through many changes. These tasks include setting up call queues and auto attendants, and setting up policies to control how calls are handled.

> **This skill covers how to:**
> - Manage resource accounts
> - Create and configure call queues
> - Create and configure auto attendants
> - Manage call park policies
> - Manage calling policies
> - Manage caller ID policies
> - Interpret the Direct Routing health dashboard

Manage resource accounts

Resource accounts are used through Microsoft 365 to represent some type of resource. In Exchange Online, these can include shared mailboxes or meeting rooms that may also be Microsoft Teams Rooms. In Microsoft Teams, these include auto attendants and call queues. These accounts are assigned the telephone numbers you wish to use for both so that PSTN users can reach them.

For both call queues and auto attendants, you need to use a virtual user license to assign to the resource account. Phone System Virtual User licenses have no cost and can be added to your tenant through the Microsoft 365 Admin Center.

You also need to acquire service numbers for call queues and auto attendants. Service numbers are just one type of number you can obtain, and were covered in Skill 2.3, "Order phone numbers." If you do not have service numbers already, make sure you order those first.

To create a resource account, do the following:

1. Log on to the TAC at *https://admin.teams.microsoft.com*.
2. In the left menu, expand **Org-wide settings** and then select **Resource accounts**.
3. Select **+Add** to create a new resource account.
4. Enter a display name and a username, and select the resource account type from the drop-down menu. In this example we are creating an auto attendant, as shown in Figure 2-28.

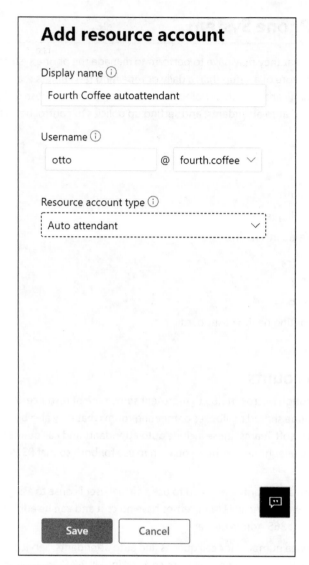

FIGURE 2-28 Creating a resource account

5. When finished, select **Save**.

6. Then, log on to the Microsoft 365 Admin Center at *https://admin.microsoft.com.*

7. Select the resource account you created, select the **Licenses and apps** tab, and assign the resource account a Microsoft 365 Phone System-Virtual User license, as shown in Figure 2-29.

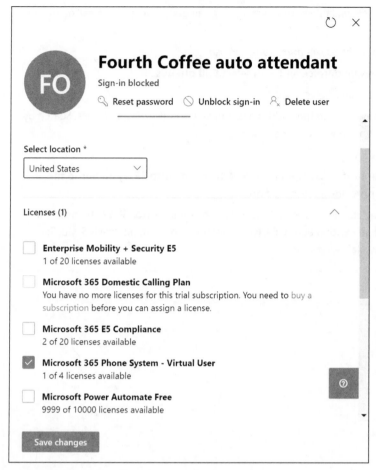

FIGURE 2-29 Assigning a license to a resource account

8. Select **Save changes**.

Create and configure call queues

Call queues are useful when you want to take inbound calls that more than one person could handle, such as inbound sales calls or a help desk. Every user who is in the queue could take the call, and calls can be distributed based on a number of options. Call queues can include the following:

- A recorded greeting message
- Music on hold
- Call routing
- Options for overflow and timeouts

You need to obtain a service number, create a resource account, assign the service number to the resource account, and, if you are using a greeting or custom music on hold, have audio files in WMA, WAV, or MP3 available before setting up a call queue. To create a call queue, do the following:

1. Log on to the TAC at *https://admin.teams.microsoft.com*.

2. In the left menu, expand **Voice** and then select **Call queues**.

3. In the **Call queues** pane, select **+Add**.

4. Give the queue a name, and then add the resource account you want to use. Search by display name, not by UPN. Then select **Add**.

5. Set the desired language.

6. If you want to use a recorded greeting, select the radio button **Play an audio file** and then upload your previously recorded greeting.

7. If you want to play custom music on hold, select the radio button **Play an audio file** and then upload an existing audio file. Note that the maximum file size is 5 MB. See Figure 2-30 for available settings.

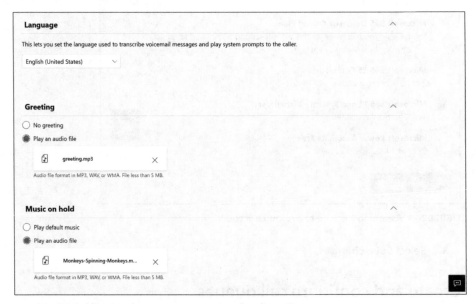

FIGURE 2-30 Configuring the resource account and audio options

8. Choose how **Call answering** will be handled. You can have calls go to a channel in a team, and everyone in the team can take the call, or you can select individual users and groups.

9. Then, choose the **Routing method** for calls. These include the following:

   a. Attendant routing—Everyone's phone rings at once, and whoever answers first gets the call.

   b. Serial routing—Starts with the first user and rings through the list one at a time until someone answers.

c. Round robin—Calls will be routed randomly within the call group, with each user getting the same number of calls.

   d. Longest idle—The user who has been the longest without a call will be rung first.

10. Enable **Presence-based routing** if you want users who are away or busy to be skipped.

11. Enable **Call agents can opt out of taking calls** if you want users to be able to decline a call and have it go to the next available, based on the routing method.

12. Set **Call agent alert time** to control how long a call tries to ring a user before it goes to the next, as shown in Figure 2-31.

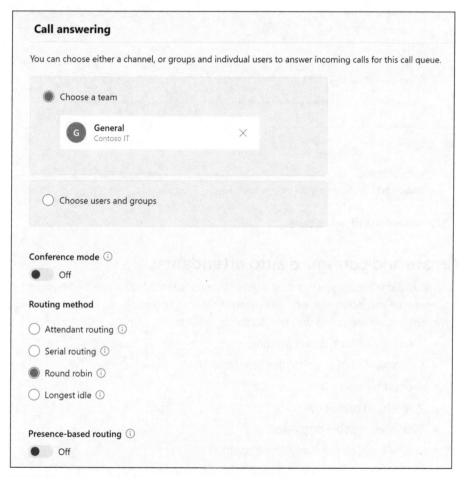

FIGURE 2-31 Setting up a call queue

13. In the **Call overflow handling** section, select the maximum number of calls in the queue, whether to disconnect or redirect calls when the maximum is reached, and call timeout handling options, as shown in Figure 2-32.

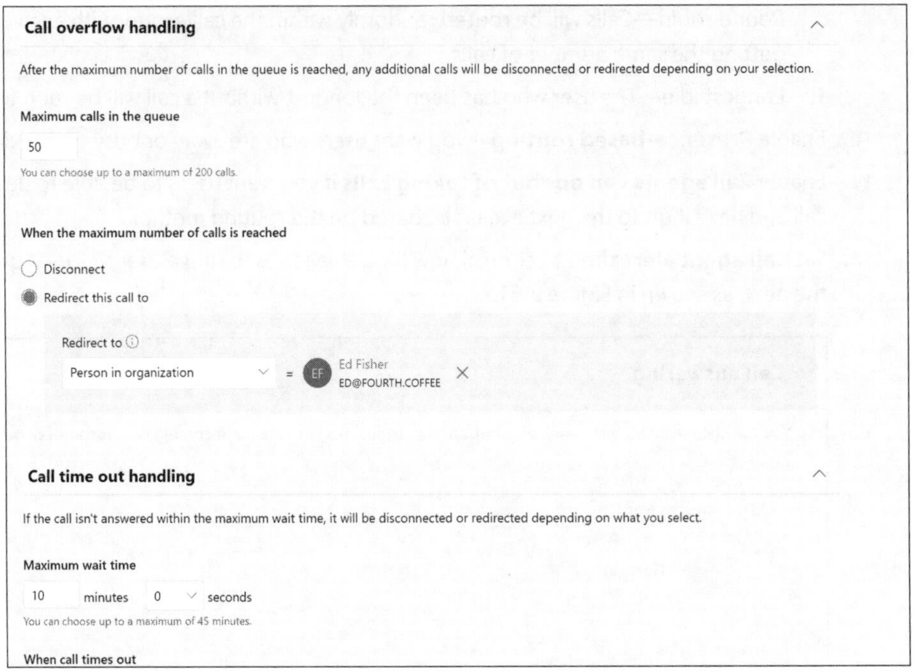

Call overflow handling   ∧

After the maximum number of calls in the queue is reached, any additional calls will be disconnected or redirected depending on your selection.

Maximum calls in the queue

50

You can choose up to a maximum of 200 calls.

When the maximum number of calls is reached

○ Disconnect

◉ Redirect this call to

Redirect to ⓘ

| Person in organization ∨ | = | EF | Ed Fisher ED@FOURTH.COFFEE | ✕ |

Call time out handling   ∧

If the call isn't answered within the maximum wait time, it will be disconnected or redirected depending on what you select.

Maximum wait time

10   minutes   0 ∨ seconds

You can choose up to a maximum of 45 minutes.

When call times out

FIGURE 2-32 Setting up a call queue, continued

14. When finished, select **Save**.

Create and configure auto attendants

Auto attendants enable you to set up a telephone number with a corresponding menu system. Both external and internal callers can listen to a recorded greeting and navigate a menu to have their call transferred to the right person or department. They have the following features:

- A recorded informational greeting
- Customized menus, which may be multilevel
- A directory search (search by name)
- A shared voice mail box
- (Optional) multiple languages
- Business and after-hours/holiday options
- Transferring a call to another person, queue, or other auto attendant

As with call queues, you must obtain a service number, create a resource account, and assign the service number to the resource account before you create the auto attendant. If you want to use a recorded message instead of text-to-speech, you want to have audio files (again, WAV, WMA, or MP3 and less than 5 MB) ready to upload.

To set up an auto attendant, follow these steps:

1. Log on to the TAC at *https://admin.teams.microsoft.com*.

2. In the left menu, expand **Voice** and then select **Auto attendants**.

3. Select **+Add** to begin.

4. Name your auto attendant.

5. If desired, set the optional operator. This can be a person, a queue, or another auto attendant.

6. Make sure to select the correct time zone for the auto attendant, as this will control when the switch from business to nonbusiness hours happens.

7. Select the language. Remember that one auto attendant can link to others, so your first may be to have the user select a language, and the next level can be in a different language from the root.

8. Choose whether to enable voice prompts. If enabled, users can say their selections rather than pressing numbers on the dial pad, such as "press or say 1." Then select **Next**.

9. In the **Call flow** panel, you first choose whether to have no greeting, a recorded greeting you will upload, or a spoken greeting that the system will read from text.

10. Next, you decide whether to hang up; redirect the call to a person, another attendant or queue, an external phone, or to voicemail; or to play a menu with options, as shown in Figure 2-33.

FIGURE 2-33 Setting up an auto attendant call flow

11. You can upload an audio file or have a text-to-speech greeting to introduce the menu, then you can create a menu. The dial key corresponds to a number on a phone's dial pad, while the Voice command is the word a caller will need to say and will be available

only if you enabled voice prompts on the prior screen. Enter the options you desire, and then select whether to enable dial by name or dial by extension, as shown in Figure 2-34.

FIGURE 2-34 Setting up an auto attendant call flow, continued

12. When finished, select **Next**.

13. Next you set up your business hours and what happens if someone calls after hours. If your business is closed on a particular day, leave the default 12:00 AM setting, as shown in Figure 2-35.

FIGURE 2-35 Setting up an auto attendant business hours

14. Configure options for **Set up after hours call flow**, and when finished, select **Next**.

15. You can set up **Holiday call settings** in advance if you want your auto attendant to do different things from what is set up in business hours. When done, select **Next**.

16. If you enabled **Dial by name** in step 11, the **Find People** pane enables you to either expose or hide specific users from being discoverable using the search. The defaults are to include all users and exclude none. Make any necessary changes and then select **Next**.

17. In the **Resource accounts** panel, add the resource account you configured for this auto attendant, and then select **Submit**.

REAL WORLD   **WHAT'S IN A NAME?**

Auto attendants are one of the few things you will create in Microsoft Teams that do not have, let alone require, a description field. You want to make sure that if you are going to have multiple auto attendants, you name them in such a way that you can easily tell which is which. However, since you will find yourself using PowerShell more and more, make sure you keep the names short, and consider whether to use spaces or concatenate the words together using CamelCase to make it easier to work with them when scripting.

Manage call park policies

Call park policies control how users can place callers on hold and transfer them to another user. You can use the Global (Org-wide default) policy for all users if you prefer or create a custom policy. When someone parks a call, it is assigned a numeric code. On another phone, the user or someone else can pick up the call by entering the numeric code that corresponds to the parked call. A timeout ensures that if if no one picks up a parked call, it rings back to the original user/phone where they were parked.

To configure call park policies, do the following:

1. Log on to the TAC at *https://admin.teams.microsoft.com*.

2. In the left menu, expand **Voice** and then select **Call park policies**.

3. To edit the **Global (Org-wide default)** policy, select it from the list and then select **Edit**.

4. Enable **Call park** by setting the switch to **On**.

5. Select **Save**.

Manage calling policies

Calling policies control the calling features available to users of Microsoft Teams who have a calling plan. As with other policies, you can use the Global (Org-wide default), you can use one of the included additional policies that either allows or disallows calling, or you can create a custom policy. The Global policy will apply to all users with calling plans and to whom another policy has not been applied. To manage calling policies, do the following:

1. Log on to the TAC at *https://admin.teams.microsoft.com*.

2. In the left menu, expand **Voice** and then select **Calling policies**.

3. Select the **Global (Org wide default)** policy and then select **Edit**.

4. Make any desired changes, as shown in Figure 2-36.

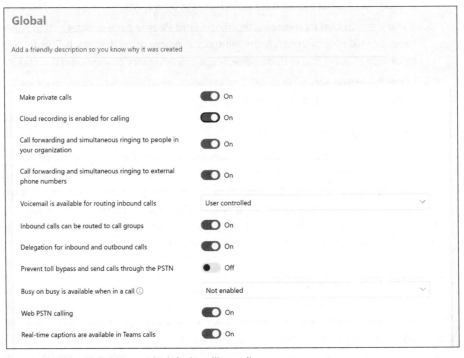

Global

Add a friendly description so you know why it was created

Make private calls	On
Cloud recording is enabled for calling	On
Call forwarding and simultaneous ringing to people in your organization	On
Call forwarding and simultaneous ringing to external phone numbers	On
Voicemail is available for routing inbound calls	User controlled
Inbound calls can be routed to call groups	On
Delegation for inbound and outbound calls	On
Prevent toll bypass and send calls through the PSTN	Off
Busy on busy is available when in a call ⓘ	Not enabled
Web PSTN calling	On
Real-time captions are available in Teams calls	On

FIGURE 2-36 The Global (Org-wide default) calling policy

5. Select **Save** when finished.

Manage caller ID policies

By default, when a Microsoft Teams user with a calling plan makes a phone call to a PSTN number, the DID assigned to the Microsoft Teams user will show up as the number displayed in the recipient's caller ID. You can override this with a caller ID policy. You may want to show your organization's main number, or a phone number assigned to a calling queue or auto attendant so that if the person calls back, their call goes to somewhere other than only the person who called them. The Global (Org-wide default) applies to all users who do not have a specific policy applied to them, and you can create multiple policies if you have different needs for different users. To manage Caller ID policies, do the following:

1. Log on to the TAC at *https://admin.teams.microsoft.com*.

2. In the left menu, expand **Voice** and then select **Caller ID policies**.

3. Select the **Global (Org-wide default)** and then select **Edit**.

4. To replace the user's phone number with the number assigned to an auto attendant, select the option **Replace the caller ID with** and choose **Service number**.

5. Then, in **Replace the caller ID with this service number** select the service number from the drop-down list that corresponds to the auto attendant or queue you wish to use, as shown in Figure 2-37.

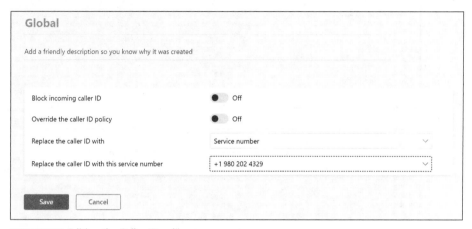

FIGURE 2-37 Editing the Caller ID policy

6. Select **Save** when done.

> **REAL WORLD** **WHAT'S IN A NAME?**
>
> Not exposed in the GUI, you can use PowerShell to set the Caller Name (CNAM) that appears in Caller ID. You can use the Set-CsCallingLineIdentity cmdlet. Try this:
>
> ```
> > $ObjOID = (Get-CsOnlineApplicationInstance -Identity UPN@domain.com).ObjectId
> ```
>
> ```
> > Set-CsCallingLineIdentity -Identity Global -CallingIDSubstitute Resource
> -ResourceAccount $ObjOID -CompanyName "*Fourth Coffee*"
> ```

Interpret the Direct Routing health dashboard

The Health Dashboard for Direct Routing enables direct routing customers to monitor the connection between Microsoft Teams and their session border controllers (SBCs). The health dashboard monitors SBCs, telephony services, and network parameters that can help you identify, troubleshoot, and resolve issues when using direct routing. If you are not using direct routing, you will not see any information in the dashboard and will encounter errors when selecting through the various panes. If you do have direct routing in place, to access the Direct Routing health dashboard, do the following:

1. Log on to the TAC at *https://admin.teams.microsoft.com*.

2. In the left menu, expand **Voice** and then select **Direct routing**; you will see a dashboard similar to what is shown in Figure 2-38.

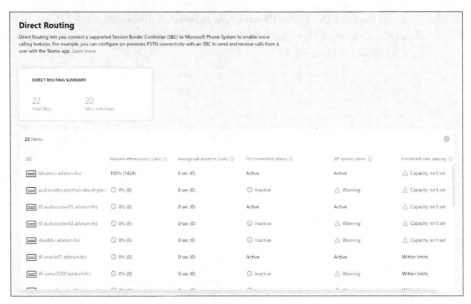

FIGURE 2-38 The Direct Routing Health Dashboard

The Direct Routing Health Dashboard includes information on the following:

- Direct Routing summary—This shows the total number of SBCs and how many (if any) have issues.

- SBC—This shows the FQDN of the SBC.

- Network Effectiveness Ratio (NER)—This shows the ratio of calls sent to calls delivered. NER = 100 x (Answered calls + User Busy + Ring no Answer + Terminal Reject Seizures)/ Total Calls and if less than 100 calls have been routed through an SBC, this number may appear very low and imply a problem where none exists. Complete more calls before placing much importance on NER.

- Average call duration.

- TLS connectivity status—Keep an eye on this, because it indicates when certificates are about to expire, which sadly is a common cause of otherwise avoidable issues.

- SIP options status—SIP options should be exchanged every minute. If they are not, it can indicate a misconfigured or malfunctioning SBC and can cause call problems.

- Details SIP options status—Select this to see details on the SIP options status.

- Concurrent calls capacity—useful if you specify a maximum number of calls an SBC can handle concurrently, to monitor for capacity issues.

You can drill down to get more information for a specific SBC by selecting it in the dashboard. You can view the following:

- TLS connectivity status

- TLS connectivity last status

- SIP options status

- SIP options last checked
- SBC status
- Concurrent call
- Network parameters, including jitter, packet loss, and latency
- NER

> **NEED MORE REVIEW?**   **DIRECT ROUTING CAN BE KEY FOR MANY CUSTOMERS**
>
> You can read more about the Health Dashboard for Direct Routing at *https://docs.microsoft.com/en-us/microsoftteams/direct-routing-health-dashboard.*

Chapter summary

In this chapter, we covered many of the aspects of deployment and management of Microsoft Teams for collaboration and calling. Some of the most important things to remember are as follows:

Chat and collaboration.

- Messaging policies control all aspects of what your users can do in ad hoc, meeting-based, and channel-based chat.
- External access is a key part of collaboration with customers, partners, and others, and can be securely set up to meet your organization's needs.
- Private channels give you a place to have content within a team that is avilable to only a subset of the users in that team and can be particulary useful if that team has external users.

Meetings

- Policies can be set to control who can do what in meetings and which capabilities are available. This may be necessary to meet specific compliance or privacy needs in your organization.
- Live events can be used to reach more people, including external audiences.
- For either, the network is the key component, and a combination of QoS and proper internet egress help to ensure a good experience.

Phone numbers

- Calling plans and direct routing are both ways to use Microsoft Teams as a complete calling solution.
- There are many types of phone numbers, and those assigned to users are set up differently from those that are assigned to automation.

Phone system

- Call queues and auto attendants can both be used to address specific automation needs.

Thought experiment

In this thought experiment, demonstrate your skills and knowledge of the topics covered in this chapter. You can find the answers in the section that follows.

Skill 2.1 Manage chat and collaboration experiences

1. You need to permit users from a partner to collaborate with your users in Microsoft Teams. You want to ensure that only users from the partner company can be added to Teams, but not users from any other organization. Where would you go to configure this restriction?

   a. Azure Security Center

   b. TAC

   c. Microsoft 365 Admin Center

   d. Azure Active Directory admin center

2. Your users need to collaborate with external users. They need to be able to use Microsoft Teams, and to be able to share files and work on them collaboratively. Which kind of access should they use?

   a. Guest user

   b. External user

   c. Active Directory user

   d. Azure Active Directory user

Skill 2.2 Manage meeting experiences

1. Your security team has determined that guest users can participate in Teams meetings but must not be able to turn on their cameras to share video. What kind of policy would you create to restrict video for guest users?

   a. Teams guest access policy

   b. Teams meeting policy

   c. Teams external sharing policy

   d. Teams client policy

2. What network protocol can help to ensure sufficient bandwidth is available on your network for a better meeting experience?

   a. TCP

   b. UDP

   c. QoS

   d. VPN

3. You want to prevent users from editing or deleting instant messages after sending them in chat. What kind of policy would you use to accomplish this?

   a. Teams Meeting Policy

   b. Group Policy

   c. Teams Client Policy

   d. Teams Messaging Policy

Skill 2.3 Manage phone numbers

1. What type of license do you need to have in order to provide a call-in number for meetings?

   a. Office 365 E3

   b. Calling Plan

   c. Audio Conferencing Plan

   d. Office 365 Meeting & Compliance Add-in

2. What do you need to configure to support sharing location information with first responders when a user dials emergency services from Microsoft Teams?

   a. Network locations

   b. PSAP

   c. Emergency locations

   d. User addresses

Skill 2.4 Manage Phone System

1. You want to have a phone number that people can dial that could ring every user in the sales organization. What type of number would you create?

   a. Audio conferencing

   b. Call queue

   c. Auto attendant

   d. Team phone number

2. You want to ensure that when an inbound call comes into the sales department, every member of the sales department gets an equal chance to answer the call. What routing method would you use?

   a. Attendant

   b. Serial

   c. Round robin

   d. Longest idle

3. You want to enable directory lookup so that callers can directly connect to people in your organization. However you do not want them to be able to directly connect to the CEO. How would you accomplish this?

   a. Hide the CEO in the GAL.

   b. You cannot. Dial By Name is an all-or-nothing feature.

   c. Assign the CEO a restricted access telephone number.

   d. Set up an exclusion in the Dial By Name setting.

Thought experiment answers

This section contains the solution to the thought experiment. Each answer explains why the answer choice is correct.

Skill 2.1 Manage chat and collaboration experiences

1. **a.** Azure Active Directory admin center

   You first enable external sharing in the Azure Management Portal. There, you can enter specific domains to permit or to deny.

2. **a.** Guest user

   You would create a guest user by inviting them to the team. External users can be invited to meetings and participate in chats, but they cannot access a team or a channel or collaborate on files within them.

Skill 2.2 Manage meeting experiences

1. **a.** Teams guest access policy

   In the Org-wide settings, Guest access, you can disable IP video for guests in meetings.

2. **c.** QoS

   Quality of service is used to provide priority access to the network and is the best answer for this question from the available choices.

3. **d.** Teams Messaging Policy

   A Messaging policy can be used to restrict editing and deleting sent messages.

Skill 2.3 Manage phone numbers

1. **c.** Audio Conferencing Plan

   An audio-conferencing plan is required, which can be purchased separately or comes with other plans, but not with any of the ones that are other answers to this question.

2. **c.** Emergency locations

   Emergency locations are created that include a physical address and can also include GPS coordinates.

Skill 2.4 Manage Phone System

1. **b.** Call queue

   A call queue can be used to ring multiple users.

2. **c.** Round robin

   Round robin ensures that every user receives the same number of inbound calls.

3. **d.** Set up an exclusion in the Dial By Name setting.

   Specific users can be included or excluded from Dial By Name.

CHAPTER 3

Manage Teams and app policies

In this chapter, we cover many of the day-to-day tasks that you will perform as a Microsoft Teams administrator. Although this is the smallest portion of the exam in terms of content, for many it may be the majority of your efforts managing Teams for your organization.

Skills covered in this chapter:

- Skill 3.1: Manage a team
- Skill 3.2: Manage membership in a team
- Skill 3.3: Implement policies for Microsoft Teams apps

Skill 3.1: Manage a team

This skill covers how to manage a team, which is useful for both administrators and team owners. This includes many of the administrative tasks related to managing Teams, except for lifecycle management, which we covered in Skill 1.3.

This skill covers how to:

- Create a team
- Upgrade an existing resource to a team
- Manage privacy levels for a team
- Manage org-wide teams
- Create and manage policy packages in Teams

Create a team

Creating a team is something that anyone in your organization should be able to do. By default, they can. Some organizations may wish to restrict this, but just as any group or department or subset of employees may come together to work on something as a team, they should be able to use Microsoft Teams to get work done, without having to engage the information technology department or open a helpdesk ticket just to get started. But since some organizations may need to restrict this, we will cover how to do so, as well as how to create teams from scratch or by using templates in both the TAC and the Teams client.

Let's first look at controlling who can create a team. By default, any licensed user in your organization can create up to 250 teams, whereas administrators can create up to 500,000 teams. This matches the limits for Microsoft 365 Groups, because each team has a corresponding group, so these limits derive from that. If you wish to limit who can create a team, you do so by limiting who can create a Microsoft 365 Group. When you do this, you limit not only groups and teams, but several other services within Microsoft 365. Specifically, these include the following:

- Outlook
- SharePoint
- Yammer
- Microsoft Teams
- Microsoft Stream (classic)
- Planner
- Power BI (classic)
- Project for the web

When you restrict who can create Microsoft 365 Groups, you create and populate a single group that has permissions to create Microsoft 365 Groups.

Once added to that group, they can create Microsoft 365 Groups that can be used across the services. Keep in mind that you cannot remove the ability for members of administrative groups, such as Global Administrators, to create Microsoft 365 Groups. To restrict who can create Microsoft 365 Groups, follow these steps:

1. Log on to the Microsoft 365 admin center at *https://admin.microsoft.com*.
2. In the left menu, expand **Groups** and select **Active Groups**.
3. Select **Add a group** and create a group. Give it an intuitive name like **M365GroupCreators**.
4. Add any users to this group, which you want to be able to create other M365 Groups, and by extension, Teams.
5. Now, access *https://docs.microsoft.com/en-us/microsoft-365/solutions/manage-creation-of-groups?view=o365-worldwide* and copy the PowerShell script from that page.
6. Edit the first line so that it matches the name of the group you created in step 3.
7. Run the script.
8. Wait at least 30 minutes for this to take effect.

Once done, you can add or remove users from the group you created to control who can create Microsoft 365 Groups and therefore new teams. Remember, administrative groups will not be limited by this and will always be able to create Microsoft 365 Groups and new teams.

Creating a new team automatically creates the Microsoft 365 Group associated with the team. Administrators can use the TAC, and users (those who have permission to create new M365 Groups) can use the Teams desktop client or web client. To create new teams from scratch using the TAC, follow these steps:

1. Log on to the TAC at *https://admin.teams.microsoft.com*.

2. In the left menu, expand **Teams** and select **Manage teams**.

3. On the **Manage teams** pane, select **+Add**.

4. Give the new team a name and a description, add one or more owners, set the sensitivity, and choose whether the team is Private or Public, as shown in Figure 3-1.

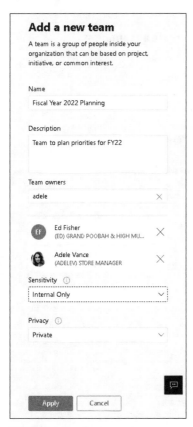

FIGURE 3-1 Creating a new team

5. When done, select **Apply**.

6. Select the team from the list of teams, and select **Edit**.

7. Expand **Conversations** and make any necessary changes to the default settings.

8. Expand **Channels** and make any necessary changes to the default settings.

9. When done, select **Apply**.

10. To add members, on the **Members** tab, select **+Add** and add members.

11. Select the **Channels** tab and add any additional channels.

12. When done, select **Apply**.

13. Note the team's email address on the details page of the team.

Your newly created team is ready to use. Unless you set it to private, users can search for the team in the client within a few moments of creating it.

Users who have permission to create new M365 Groups can also create new teams right in the Microsoft Teams client or the web interface. The steps are the same:

1. Log on to **Teams**.

2. In the left menu, select **Teams**.

3. At the bottom of the Teams list, select **Join or create a team**.

4. Select **Create a team**, as shown in Figure 3-2.

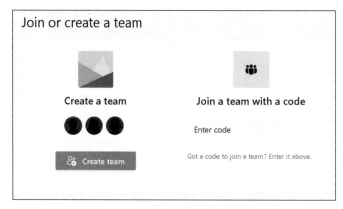

FIGURE 3-2 Creating a new team in the Teams client

5. On the next screen, you can choose whether to create a new team from scratch or from an existing Microsoft 365 Group or team, or you can choose from an available template, as shown in Figure 3-3.

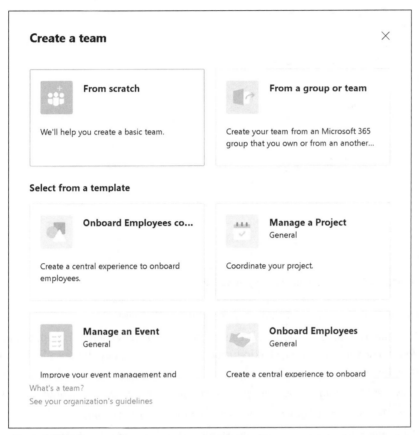

FIGURE 3-3 Options for creating a new team using the client

6. Since we discussed templates in Skill 1.3, and we will go over upgrading an existing resource to a team in the next section, here select **From scratch**.

7. In the next window, set the team's **Sensitivity** if prompted, and choose whether to create a **Private**, a **Public**, or an **Org-wide** team. (Note that Org-wide teams can be used for organizations with no more than 10,000 users.) For this walk-through, select **Public**. Note the description of each type of team, as shown in Figure 3-4.

FIGURE 3-4 Setting the kind of team you want to create

8. Give your team a name and a description, then select **Create**.

9. The team is created and you are then prompted to add new users or groups to the team. You can do this now, or select **Skip** to come back to it later, or to let users find and join a public team on their own.

You may want to configure the team you just created with any specific settings. To do this:

1. In the Teams UI, scroll down to and select the team you just created.

2. Select the ellipsis button to the right of the team name, and select **Manage team**. You will see a screen like the one shown in Figure 3-5.

FIGURE 3-5 Settings for a team

3. You will see six tabs available. On the **Members** tab, you can add additional owners, members, and guests.

4. Select the **Channels** tab and create any required channels in addition to the default General channel.

5. Select the **Settings** tab to add a team picture, set permissions, and control other settings, as shown in Figure 3-6.

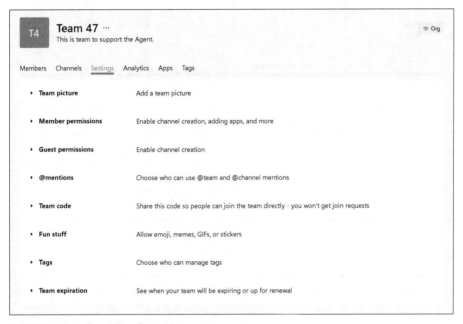

FIGURE 3-6 Specific settings for a team

6. Select the **Analytics** tab to see analytics on the team, including size and usage. This data will start to populate after you add users and content and people start to collaborate.

7. Select the **Apps** tab to see the apps that are already used by your team. You can select **More apps** to add more if necessary.

8. Finally, select the **Tags** tab to create any tags you want to use with this team.

When done, you can simply select the General channel or any other part of the Teams UI. There is no **Exit** or **Apply** button.

Upgrade an existing resource to a team

Remember that Microsoft Teams is tightly integrated with and uses both Microsoft 365 Groups and SharePoint sites. While you will probably start with creating a team from scratch or by using a template, which in turn will create a Microsoft 365 Group (M365 Group) and a SharePoint site for you, you can take an existing M365 Group or SharePoint site and create a team from them if you wish. There is more than one way to do this.

To create a team from a Microsoft 365 Group using the admin center, follow these steps:

1. Log on to the Microsoft 365 admin center at *https://admin.microsoft.com*.

2. In the left menu, expand **Groups** and select **Active groups**.

3. Find the existing group you wish to use and select the name.

4. In the properties of the group, select the **Microsoft Teams** tab.

5. Select **Create a team**, as shown in Figure 3-7.

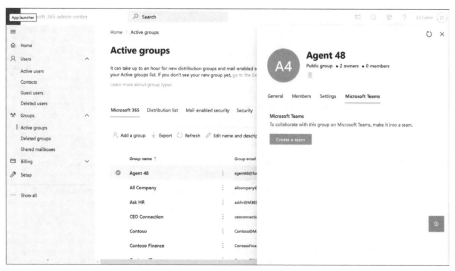

FIGURE 3-7 Creating a team from a Microsoft 365 Group in the Microsoft 365 Group admin center

6. Select **Create a team** to confirm. This will create the team and the corresponding SharePoint site.

7. You can now manage this team in the client app or in the TAC.

REAL WORLD   **THIS PROBABLY ISN'T WHAT YOU'RE GOING TO DO**

Although it is possible to create a team from a Microsoft 365 Group at some point after the group has been created, when you create a new Microsoft 365 Group the default selection is to go ahead and create a team for that group. Still, it's good to know how to do this for existing, likely older, Microsoft 365 Groups.

To create a team from an existing SharePoint site, do the following:

1. Log on to SharePoint and access the SharePoint site you wish to use.

2. On the right hand side of the SharePoint site, scroll down until you see **Add real-time chat**, as shown in Figure 3-8.

FIGURE 3-8 Creating a team from a SharePoint site

3. Select **Continue**.

4. Select any of the offered SharePoint resources to pin, and then select **Add Teams**.

5. Select **Go to Teams** to access the new team and manage any further settings.

To create a team from an existing resource within Teams, do the following:

1. In the Teams UI, select the **Teams** tab, and then select **Join or create a team**.

2. Select **Create a team**.

3. Select **From a group or team**.

4. In the **Create a new team from something you already own** pane, choose **Team** if you want to clone an existing team, or choose **Microsoft 365 group** to create a team from a group. In this example, select **Microsoft 365 group**, as shown in Figure 3-9.

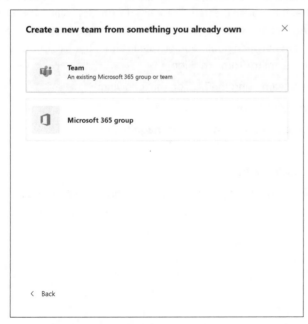

FIGURE 3-9 Creating a team from a Microsoft 365 Group or existing team

5. The next pane will show you all Microsoft 365 Groups in your tenant that do not already have a team associated with them. Choose the group you wish to use, and then select **Create**.

6. As with the previous approaches, you can then manage the team as normal in the Teams UI.

Manage privacy levels for a team

Privacy levels for teams within Microsoft Teams control the membership of a team. No matter what the privacy level of a team, only members of the team can see what is in the team. However, how someone becomes a member is controlled by the privacy level. There are three privacy levels in Microsoft Teams:

1. Public: Anyone in your organization can join.

2. Private: Only team owners can add members.

3. Org-wide: Everyone in your organization will be automatically added.

EXAM TIP

Org-wide teams can only be created by Global Admins, are only available to orgs with fewer than 10,000 users, and an organization cannot have more than five total org-wide teams. The following are not added to an org-wide team: accounts blocked from sign-in, guest users, resource accounts, room or equipment accounts, or shared mailbox accounts.

You can set the privacy level for a team when you create it, and you can change the privacy level for a team at any point after it has been created. Changing the privacy level does not change existing membership. Any team owner, Teams admin, or Global Administrator can change the privacy level for a team between public and private in either the TAC or the UI, but they must use the UI to change a team to/from org-wide.

To manage privacy levels for a team using the TAC, do the following:

1. Log on to the TAC at *https://admin.teams.microsoft.com*.

2. In the left menu, expand **Teams** and then select **Manage teams**.

3. Find the team in the list and select it.

4. In the upper-right corner, select **Edit**.

5. Select the new privacy level from the drop-down menu, as shown in Figure 3-10.

FIGURE 3-10 Creating a team from a Microsoft 365 Group or existing team

6. Select **Apply** when done.

Manage org-wide teams

Org-wide teams are available for organizations that have fewer than 10,000 users and automatically include all users in the organization. Memberships are automatically updated when new users are created. Organizations with fewer than 10,000 users can create up to five org-wide teams.

Newer tenants will have an org-wide team created automatically for them when the tenant is instantiated that is named for the tenant, whereas older tenants will not have a default org-wide team but can, of course, create one themselves. At this time, only Global Admins can create/manage org-wide teams, and they must use the Teams UI to do so; they cannot use the TAC. Users are automatically added to org-wide teams and cannot remove themselves from an org-wide team. Unlicensed users are included and will automatically be assigned a Teams Exploratory license when they first access the org-wide team.

NEED MORE REVIEW? **WHAT ARE TEAMS EXPLORATORY LICENSES?**

See *https://docs.microsoft.com/en-us/microsoftteams/teams-exploratory* for more information on the Teams Exploratory license.

There are several recommendations for managing org-wide teams, based on the fact that these teams include everyone in your organization. You can specify these in the settings for the team. They include the following:

- Allow only team owners to post to the General channel. By default, Global Admins and Teams admins are owners, and an admin can assign additional owners. Keeping the General channel limited to a few authorized posters ensures that only information that is really relevant to the entire organization can be posted.

- Turn off @mentions to reduce the notifications that go out to all users.

- Automatically show important channels if you have more than just the General channel to ensure all users see them.

- Set up channel moderation so that owners, or others given the moderation role, can ensure that posts to the General or other channels are appropriate.

- Remove accounts that might not belong; there may be some that are automatically added but should not be, such as user accounts assigned to external consultants or used by service accounts.

REAL WORLD   **PLEASE SIR, I WANT SOME MORE**

Although the 10,000 user limit may be increased in the future, for now it is a hard limit. Organizations with more than 10,000 users are encouraged to look at using Yammer for org-wide purposes. Consider whether to create more than one org-wide team, or to add channels to the first org-wide team, as the team is literally org-wide. You want to make it easy for your entire organization to find what they need without creating too much sprawl.

Create and manage policy packages in Teams

A Teams policy package is a collection of policies and settings that can be assigned to users and that controls many aspects of using Teams, including what features are available. Microsoft Teams includes several policy packages by default, and admins can edit existing policy packages or create their own if an included one does not suit the organization's needs. Policy packages are meant to simplify role-based management of teams but not to meet any specific compliance or regulatory requirements, though you may use them to meet those requirements if desired.

To create and manage policy packages in Teams, do the following:

1. Log on to the TAC at *https://admin.teams.microsoft.com*.
2. In the left menu, select **Policy packages**.
3. On the **Manage packages** tab, you will see the packages that are included by default.
4. You can create a new policy package by selecting the **+Add** button.
5. You can then add existing policies from each of the categories, as shown in Figure 3-11.

FIGURE 3-11 Creating a new policy package

6. Add each of the policies you want in your policy package, and then select **Save**.

7. Select the **Group package assignment** tab.

8. Select the **+Add group** button.

9. Find the group to which you wish to apply the policy package, and then select the policy package, as shown in Figure 3-12.

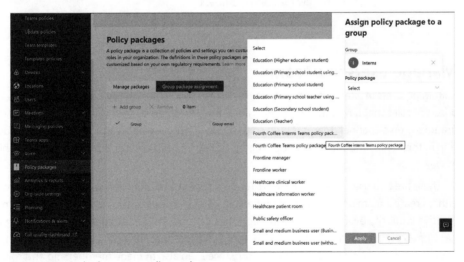

FIGURE 3-12 Assigning a new policy package

10. Edit the ranking if necessary, and then select **Apply**.

Skill 3.2: Manage membership in a team

It's commonly said that the only constant is change, and when it comes to Teams, one thing you can count on is that membership in most teams will, at some point, need to change. Whether that is handled by team owners or by admins is up to you, but whether configuring the initial membership, automating membership, or reviewing membership, managing membership in a team is an important and frequent task.

> **This skill covers how to:**
> - Manage users in a team
> - Configure dynamic membership
> - Manage access review for team members

Manage users in a team

Managing users in a team is about more than simply adding or removing users. There are different roles that have different permissions, and these can be set broadly on a team or more granularly on a channel. Teams is built so that non-IT team owners can manage the membership in their team and the roles people have, but admins can and sometimes need to do this as well.

There are two user roles in Microsoft Teams: Owners and Members. Owners are users who either create a team or are assigned ownership of an existing team, and they have full administrative authority over that team. Although they cannot set things that a Teams Administrator has turned off or disabled for the service, they can make specific settings on their team, including more restrictive settings, when necessary. They can also manage membership and roles within their team. Members can participate in a team and post to any channels within the team unless an owner has restricted them. Table 3-1 provides more detail about what owners and members can do.

TABLE 3-1 Team roles

Task	Owners	Members
Create a team	Yes[1]	n/a
Join a team	Yes, unless the privacy level is set to Private	Yes, unless the privacy level is set to Private
Leave a team	Yes	Yes[1]
Edit the team name or description	Yes	No
Delete a team	Yes	No
Add a standard channel	Yes	Yes[1]
Edit a standard channel name or description	Yes	Yes[1]
Delete a standard channel	Yes	Yes[1]
Add a private channel	Yes	Yes[1]
Edit a private channel name or description	Yes	Yes[1]
Delete a private channel	Yes	No
Add members	Yes	Yes[2]
Request to add members	N/A	Yes
Add apps	Yes	Yes[1]

[1] *Unless otherwise restricted.*
[2] *Only public teams, where anyone can join.*

NEED MORE REVIEW?   WHAT ABOUT GUESTS?

Guests are not considered a role, but they can perform certain tasks in a team. For more in information, refer to Chapter 1, and see *https://docs.microsoft.com/en-us/microsoftteams/guest-experience*.

A team can have up to 100 owners, and it's important to ensure that there are at least two owners to every team, in case someone changes roles or leaves the organization. Orphaned teams cannot be managed until an administrator assigns a new owner. If a team has no owners, members can continue to use the team, and no content will be lost, but any changes to the team require an owner. A Global Admin or Teams admin can use the TAC to change a member to an owner, or they can use the Microsoft 365 Admin Center to add a new owner to the Microsoft 365 Group associated with the team.

Team owners can also set a team or a channel within a team to be moderated. Moderators can create new posts in channels, including the General channel, and can also control whether members can reply to posts, as well as whether or not bots or connectors can create messages. Moderators are important in teams with larger numbers of members, such as org-wide teams, or teams where you may wish to limit what is posted in the General channel while using other channels in the team for more open, though focused, communications. The General channel can be set so that only owners can post, and other channels can be moderated. To manage moderation, do the following:

1. Log on to the Microsoft Teams UI and select the team you wish to modify.
2. To limit posts to the General channel to owners only, select the ellipsis button next to the General channel, and select **Manage channel**.
3. Select the radio button **Only owners can post messages**, as shown in Figure 3-13.

FIGURE 3-13 Limiting the General channel to owners only

4. To set a channel for moderation, select another channel in the team, select the ellipsis button, and select **Manage channel**.
5. On the **Channel settings** tab, from the **Channel moderation** drop-down, select **On**, as shown in Figure 3-14.

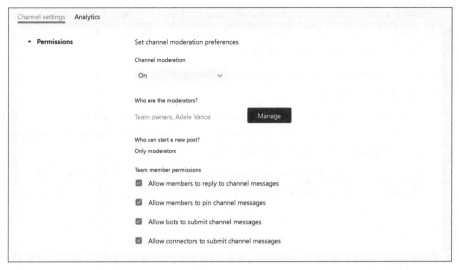

FIGURE 3-14 Enabling moderation and adding a user

6. By default, team owners are moderators. Select the **Manage** button to add additional moderators. Note that you can only add an existing member of the team to be a moderator.

7. Select **Done**.

Configure dynamic membership

Dynamic membership can automatically update team membership based on an attribute in Azure Active Directory, either synchronized from on-premises Active Directory or set directly on cloud-only accounts. When the appropriate attribute is populated, a user is added to the Microsoft 365 Group associated with a team, and if the attribute is changed or cleared, the user is removed. Dynamic membership enables you to automatically maintain membership (though not ownership) for larger teams or those focused on a specific role or job or other common element in your organization.

When using dynamic membership, it's important to note the following:

- You can only use dynamic membership rules to define membership.

- Owners can not add or remove members.

- The Teams client will hide all settings related to team membership in the UI. Admins will have to manage team owners in the TAC.

To create a team that will use dynamic membership, you first create a dynamic Microsoft 365 Group, and then you create a team from that group. To do this, follow these steps:

1. Log on to the Azure AD Admin center.

2. In the left menu, select **All services** and then select **Groups**.

3. Select **+New group**.

4. In the **New Group** pane, select **Microsoft 365** from the **Group type** drop-down. Enter a group name, email address, and description. From the **Membership type** drop-down, select **Dynamic User**, as shown in Figure 3-15.

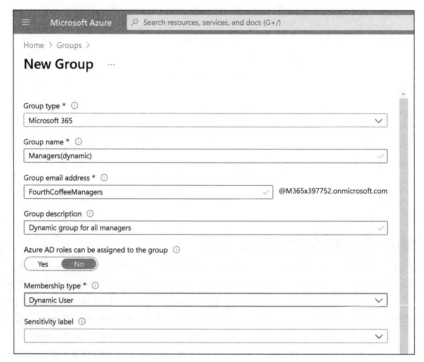

FIGURE 3-15 Creating a dynamic group

5. Add one or more owners; then select the **Add dynamic query** link.

6. In the **Dynamic membership rules** pane, select **+Add expression** or **+Get custom extension properties** to create the rule(s) that define the group membership. You can evaluate an attribute in AzureAD, such as *department*, or you can query custom extension properties from an application in your Azure AD. In this example, we are evaluating *jobTitle* and if it equals *Management*, then the rule applies, as shown in Figure 3-16.

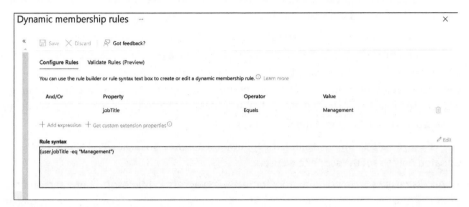

FIGURE 3-16 Creating a membership rule

7. Add any other expression or property you need to evaluate, using the AND or the OR expression as necessary. When done, select **Save**.

8. Select **Create** to finish.

Then, create a new team from the newly created group, as we reviewed in Skill 3.1.

REAL WORLD **IT'S NEVER QUITE THIS SIMPLE**

Although creating dynamic groups is very straightforward, you need to ensure that your provisioning system is consistently updating the attributes, and if a user changes jobs or departments or locations or whatever else is being evaluated, that these changes are reflected in Azure AD in a timely fashion. In the previous example, it's assumed that all managers will have the jobTitle attribute populated with "Management." If that is being handled through automation you should be fine, but if a user account is manually updated and the person mistypes, that user will not be added to the dynamic group and therefore not become a member of the appropriate team. Since team membership based on dynamic groups cannot be manually updated, you are dependent on the data in Azure AD being correct, and that may in turn be dependent on data in the on-premises Active Directory being correct, which may in turn be dependent on data in the human resources application being correct.

Manage access reviews for team members

In Skill 1.4 we introduced the concept of access reviews. If you recall, access reviews can be used to schedule and enforce a review of users' access to resources, requiring resource owners to take actions and automating actions if they do not, such as removing access. In Skill 1.4 that was in the context of guest access, but access reviews are just as important and useful when reviewing what access internal users have.

A periodic review of *who* has access to *what* is a critical part of ensuring that an organization's data is properly secured. People change roles, move off one project and on to another, and may still have access to data that they no longer have a need to access. Access reviews can ensure that permissions are reviewed periodically, helping to ensure that a user's access is removed when it is no longer needed or appropriate, whether that user is a guest of your organization or a member of the organization.

In case you are skipping around, the following content from Skill 1.4 is included here, updated only to set the scope to all users.

Access reviews are a powerful tool for reviewing access to Microsoft Teams and other corporate resources. These can be scheduled automatically to force a review of who has access to what, both to ensure that access is still valid, and that the people with access still have a need. Access reviews are an Azure AD Premium Plan 2 feature and require either a Global Administrator or a User administrator to initiate an access review in the Azure AD portal. They can assign any team owner to review the access to their team. To create an access review for all users in all teams, do the following:

1. Log on to the Azure AD portal at *https://portal.azure.com*.

2. In the Search box, enter **Identity Governance** and press Enter.

3. In the left menu, select **Access reviews**.

4. Select **+New access review** to begin.

5. In the first screen, select **Teams + Groups**, and then select the radio button next to **Select teams + groups.** Select the **Select group(s)** link and select the group or groups you want to review. Set the review scope to **All users** then select **Next: Reviews**. This is shown in Figure 3-17.

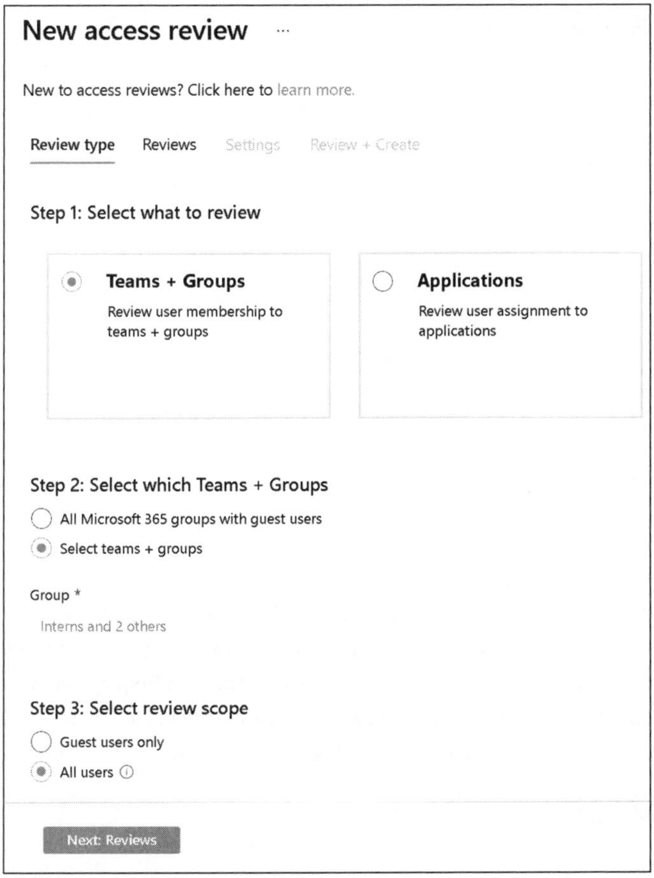

FIGURE 3-17 Settings for guest access review

6. On this screen, you can select who is to perform the review and how often they should do this. If all Microsoft 365 Groups have owners, you can select **Group owner(s)** to assign the reviews automatically. You can also select a fallback reviewer if any group no longer has an owner.

7. Then select the frequency, the duration (how long the reviewer has to complete the review), and if you wish the cycle of review to end at a specific date or after a specific number of iterations. When finished, select **Next: Settings**. Example review options are shown in Figure 3-18.

FIGURE 3-18 Additional settings for access review

8. On the next screen, you can set actions and responses based on results or lack of response by the group owner, as well as provide additional information to the reviewer, such as the last time a user actually accessed the content. This can help a reviewer determine if the guest's access is still being used. Examples are shown in Figure 3-19. When you are satisfied with the settings, select **Next: Review + Create**.

FIGURE 3-19 Additional settings for guest access review

9. You can review or make changes on the final screen, and then select **Create** when done. It may take a few moments before the access review you created will show up in the main Access review console.

You can create multiple access reviews if necessary and adjust them through the Azure portal if assigned reviewers need to change or if you need to revise the frequency or actions. By completing periodic access reviews, you help reduce the chance that someone has access to data thst they no longer need.

Skill 3.3: Implement policies for Microsoft Teams apps

Apps are an important part of the Microsoft Teams infrastructure. They enable users to extend the functionality of Teams by pulling in content connecting services that can enrich Teams, integrate line-of-business applications, use chat to communicate with bots, collaborate with others, and more. Managing apps is an important part of administering Microsoft Teams.

This skill covers how to:

- Manage org-wide app settings
- Create and manage app permission policies
- Create and manage app setup policies
- Manage app store customization

Manage org-wide app settings

Org-wide app settings are a part of managing apps in Microsoft Teams. These control whether third-party apps are allowed and whether custom apps can be published.

To manage org-wide app settings, do the following:

1. Log on to the TAC at *https://admin.teams.microsoft.com*.
2. In the left menu, expand **Team apps** and then select **Manage apps**.
3. In the **Manage apps** panel, in the upper-right corner of the panel, select **Org-wide app settings**.
4. You can make settings changes, as shown in Figure 3-20.

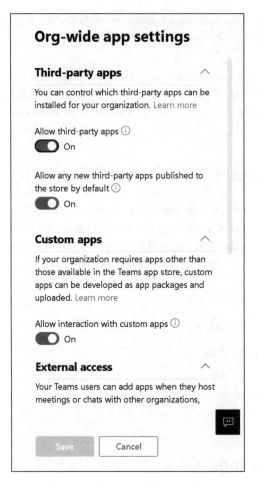

FIGURE 3-20 Managing org-wide app settings

5. If you make any changes, select **Save** to save them and exit.

REAL WORLD **NOTE THE NOTE ABOUT EXTERNAL ACCESS**

Assuming you permit guest access to Teams, then any apps one of your users adds to a team will be accessible by any guest users who have access to that team. If those apps have access to confidential or sensitive information and do not have further permission checks, then guest users may be able to access information. Consider this when permitting guest access, and check with all apps to ensure that they do proper enforcement of rights.

Create and manage app permission policies

App permission policies are used to control what apps are available to users in your tenant. You can use the default Global (Org-wide default) policy to apply to all users, or you can create additional policies if you want to make different Teams applications available to different groups of users. The Global policy will apply to all users who do not have another policy applied to them.

Because apps can provide so much more functionality to Teams, the default settings in the Global policy are to permit all apps. You can leave this in place or modify the policy to either explicitly permit some apps while blocking all others or explicitly block some apps while permitting all others. These settings can be applied separately to apps available through the Microsoft app store or to custom apps you or your developers may upload to your tenant.

To modify the Global policy, do the following:

1. Log on to the TAC at *https://admin.teams.microsoft.com*.
2. In the left menu, expand **Teams apps** and then select **Permission policies**.
3. Select the **Global (Org-wide default)** policy and then select **Edit**.
4. For each of the three settings, **Microsoft apps**, **Third-party apps**, and **Custom apps**, select the policy setting you wish to apply from the drop-down menu. If you choose to explicitly permit or block apps, you must then select the **Allow apps** or the **Block apps** button and add the apps you wish to specify, as shown in Figure 3-21.

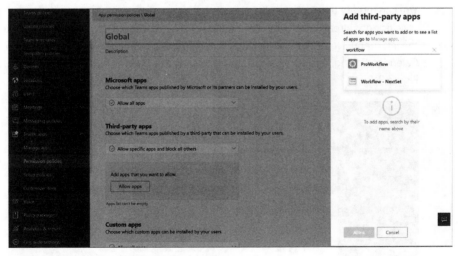

FIGURE 3-21 Permitting specific third-party apps

5. Select **Save** when done.
6. If you created a custom policy, select it and then select **Manage users** to assign it to specific groups.

Create and manage app setup policies

App setup policies are used to "push" apps to users and also to determine what appears in the left navigation bar of the client. As with other policies, you can use a single Global default policy if you want to give all users the same experience, or you can create multiple policies and assign them to users in Microsoft 365 Groups.

Microsoft Teams includes a Global (Org-wide default) policy and a policy for first-line workers (FLWs). The FirstLineWorker policy automatically pins apps relevant to FLWs, including the Shifts app. It cannot be modified, so you will probably want to create a similar policy for your FLWs if you want to pin additional apps for them.

To modify the Global policy for your tenant, do the following:

1. Log on to the TAC at *https://admin.teams.microsoft.com.*

2. In the left menu, expand **Teams apps** and select **Setup policies**.

3. Select the **Global (Org-wide default)** policy and then select **Edit**.

4. You can modify the Global policy to permit custom apps, to block user pinning, to pin specific apps already in the tenant, and to set the order in which pinned apps are in the left menu. Note that the core functions of Teams, including Activity, Chat, Teams, Calendar, Calling, and Files, are all simply apps that are pinned by default, as shown in Figure 3-22.

FIGURE 3-22 Pinned apps in the Global app setup policy

5. Select **+Add apps** to add any additional apps. Use the **Move up** or **Move down** button to sort as desired.

6. Select **Save** to save your changes and exit.

REAL WORLD   **TIME FOR A CUP (OR FOUR) OF COFFEE**

It may take a few hours before you will see pinned apps update for users affected by the policy. Patience is a virtue, and coffee is your friend.

Manage app store customization

Finally, we come to app store customization. The app store is what users will use in Teams, using the client or the web interface, where they can find apps to add and pin. Organizations can customize the app store to include their corporate logo, add a custom background, and change the color of the app store.

To customize the appearance of the app store, do the following:

1. Log on to the TAC at *https://admin.teams.microsoft.com*.

2. In the left menu, expand **Teams apps** and then select **Customize store**.

3. Customize the appearance by uploading your organization logo, logo mark, and background, and by setting the color of your organization name as desired. You can change any, or all, of these.

4. When finished, select **Save**. Note the message that is displayed stating it may be 24 hours before changes will appear to clients.

Chapter summary

In this chapter, we covered the following:

- How to manage teams
- How to manage the membership of teams
- How to control the app store experience, including customization of apps and appearance

Organizations that permit their users to be team owners, to create their own teams, and to manage the membership of their teams may find their admins do not spend much time doing any of this, except perhaps for customizing the app store. Organizations that tightly control the creation and management of Microsoft 365 Groups, and who want to approve all apps available to users, may spend significant time on these tasks. Being familiar with what is possible, both for the exam and to know what options are available to your organization, is well worth the time spent to understand these settings.

Thought experiment

In this thought experiment, demonstrate your skills and knowledge of the topics covered in this chapter. You can find the answers in the section that follows.

Skill 3.1 Manage a team

1. Your organization previously created several SharePoint sites that now should have persistent chat capabilities. What is the best way to provide this functionality?

   a. Upgrade the SharePoint sites to communications hubs.

   b. Use the SharePoint Admin Center to provision a persistent chat.

   c. Upgrade the existing SharePoint site to Teams.

   d. Apply a Teams template to the site.

2. Management wants a team to include all 6,000 employees so that they can post organization-wide announcements. They want to ensure that only certain individuals can post. What setting controls this?

   a. Team templates

   b. TAC, Teams, Manage teams, Settings

   c. Teams Client, Team, Permissions, Moderation

   d. Teams Client, Team, General Channel, Channel settings

Skill 3.2 Manage membership in a team

1. Management wants you to make sure each new hire is automatically added to their department's teams. What is the easiest way to do this?

   a. Using team templates

   b. Scheduling a PowerShell script

   c. Using Dynamic Microsoft 365 Groups

   d. Assigning a task to each team's owner

2. You need to review the membership of all teams on a quarterly basis to ensure memberships are still appropriate. What would you use to automate and delegate this?

   a. Azure AD access reviews

   b. Microsoft 365 Group audit

   c. TAC, Teams, Manage teams

   d. TAC, Analytics and reports

3. What users can add additional members to a private team?

   a. Only Teams administrators and Global Administrators

   b. Only the team's owners

    c. Teams administrators, Global Administrators, and the team's owners

    d. The team's owners and current members

Skill 3.3 Implement policies for Microsoft Teams apps

1. You need to restrict users from being able to use third-party apps. Where in the TAC would you go to set this?

    a. Org-wide settings, App settings

    b. Teams apps, Customize store

    c. Teams, Teams policies

    d. Teams apps, Permission policies

2. Where do you go in the TAC to ensure every user has a specific app pinned to the sidebar in Teams?

    a. Org-wide settings, Teams settings, Client

    b. Users, UX settings

    c. Teams apps, Setup policies

    d. Teams, Manage teams

Thought experiment answers

This section contains the solution to the thought experiment. Each answer explains why the answer choice is correct.

Skill 3.1 Manage a team

1.   **c.** Upgrade the existing SharePoint site to Teams

   You can create a new team from an existing resource such as a SharePoint site or a Microsoft 365 Group.

2.   **d.** Teams Client, Team, General Channel, Channel settings

   You can configure a channel to only permit owners to post messages. You need to use the Teams client to set this.

Skill 3.2 Manage membership in a team

1.   **c.** Dynamic Microsoft 365 Groups

   When you create a Microsoft 365 Group, and a team from that group, membership to the team is automatically assigned to all members of the group.

2.   **a.** Azure AD Access Reviews

   Azure AD Access Reviews are used to automatically schedule and assign reviews of access to resources, including Microsoft Teams.

3.   **c.** Teams administrators, Global Administrators, and the team's owners

Members of a private team can request that someone else becomes a member, but only owners, Teams administrators, or Global Administrators can add them.

Skill 3.3 Implement policies for Microsoft Teams apps

1.   **d.** Teams apps, Permission policies

You can configure Teams apps Permission policies to allow all, block all, allow specific, or block specific apps for Microsoft apps, third-party apps, and custom apps.

2.   **c.** Teams apps, Setup policies

Teams apps Setup policies control what apps are automatically pinned to the menu bar, including the order in which they are displayed.

Index

M

N

U

V - Z

Plug into learning at

MicrosoftPressStore.com

The Microsoft Press Store by Pearson offers:

- Free U.S. shipping

- Buy an eBook, get three formats – Includes PDF, EPUB, and MOBI to use with your computer, tablet, and mobile devices

- Print & eBook Best Value Packs

- eBook Deal of the Week – Save up to 50% on featured title

- Newsletter – Be the first to hear about new releases, announcements, special offers, and more

- Register your book – Find companion files, errata, and product updates, plus receive a special coupon* to save on your next purchase

 Pearson